PLAYING BALL

PLAYING BALL

LIFE LESSONS FROM MY JOURNEY TO THE SUPER BOWL AND BEYOND

VERNON DAVIS

www.kensingtonbooks.com

DAFINA BOOKS are published by

Kensington Publishing Corp.
900 Third Ave.
New York, NY 10022

ISBN: 978-1-4967-4657-3
First Kensington Hardcover Edition: September 2024

ISBN: 978-1-4967-4659-7 (ebook)

Library of Congress Control Number: 2024936505

10 9 8 7 6 5 4 3 2 1

Printed in the United States of America

To my mother and grandparents,
With love,
Vernon Davis

Contents

Introduction

I Was Just Trying to Help Vernon . . .

WHEN WE DRAFTED VERNON DAVIS, I THOUGHT, *MAN, THIS GUY is going to be a beast! He's really going to be a difference maker. He's going to make a difference for the team right away. He's going to be a game changer!*

When you looked at Vernon coming out of college, with his size, he was this big guy, with huge hands, and he ran like a deer. And I'm, like, *Wow! Teams have to account for this guy every time he lines up.* So, I just thought of nothing but positivity.

I thought—if the right circumstances were in place—that he would be a real standout player for us. At the time, I didn't know much about him as a person. I just know that when we drafted him, he was so excited that he cried. He was just overjoyed that, you know, the San Francisco 49ers had selected him in the NFL Draft.

In fact, Vernon was one of *two* first-round picks we had that year. Manny Lawson, a linebacker, was taken as the other pick. So, it was a fantastic day for the 49ers, and I just thought, *I'm excited to see what other intangibles he's going to bring to the team.*

INTRODUCTION

As soon as we got him on the field, we could all see that he was passionate and fiery, with an edge to him. You know, Vernon was one of those guys who, if you rubbed him the wrong way or he thought you had disrespected him, pushed his buttons, or hit him wrong at practice—oh, it was *on*! I mean, he was that guy who you always had to ask, "Hey, man, what's your problem? Let's get back to the huddle."

And Vernon would say, "No, man. This dude here is in my face."

So, every day at practice, you almost had to break up a fight with Vernon. He was kind of disruptive, in a way. Some of that behavior you *like* as a coach. You know, you liked how seriously he took the game. He was an excellent blocker too. And I kept thinking, *You know what? He's one of the better blockers we have on the team.* That was a realization we came to as soon as we drafted him.

Well, I figured that was a great add-on, but blocking was not why we drafted him. We wanted Vernon to be a downfield threat to catch the football. I mean, this kid could bust the game wide open. But that deep ball threat seemed to be missing more times than not. We could all see *glimpses* of it. However, it never fully took place early on with Vernon. So, we were still waiting for him to develop.

Now, during that time—early on, when Vernon was first on the team and in our locker rooms and facilities—we had a conversation when Head Coach Mike Nolan was still there. I was still the linebackers' coach at the time. I would say to Vernon, "You're making it very difficult for Coach Nolan to really get things done here at practice. You're being so disruptive that every time we turn around, there's nearly a fight. I mean, you just have to forget about some of these things people say to you and get back to *practice*, man."

Vernon would look at you and kind of process it all, and say, "Okay, Coach. I got you."

INTRODUCTION

You know, he was always respectful. "Yes, sir. No, sir," and all of that. But the next day, the same thing would happen with another teammate. So, on the first day that I became head coach, I pulled Vernon aside.

I told him, "Vernon, now look, I've been talking to you as an assistant coach, but now I'm talking to you as *head* coach. I need you to help me turn this thing around. I need all the leadership I can get."

I said to him, "All the talent you have, that's *great*. But now I need you to turn that talent into *skill*. And I need your attitude to come with it. I'm not going to tolerate anything less than that. If you can't do that, we're going to have a problem."

I told him all that, and he looked at me once again and said, "Okay, Coach."

I was really trying to set up a new relationship between us, you know. And I told him, "Hey, man, I know you can be a great player. I know you can help this team get over the hump. I *know* you can."

In turn, he was saying everything I wanted to hear. "Okay, Coach. I got you. I know I can be good."

In retrospect, I don't think he took what I was telling him to *heart*. He was just responding to that *moment*. I thought to myself, *This is the kind of guy who if I say something, I have to be a man of my word. I'm not going to say something and not do it.* But I don't think Vernon understood me at that magnitude. I had to set a precedent for the team that I *meant* what I said.

So, when Vernon got the penalty against Seattle, I was okay with it at first. It happens. We *all* get penalties. But he came over to the sideline after the referee called the penalty on him—which was obvious to everyone in the arena—and Vernon started eyeing the ref and saying, "That's bullcrap! You know I didn't do nothing to that guy, man. I didn't do nothing. He was talking crap *to me.*"

So, I said, "Vernon, come on to the sideline, man."

You know, the play was already over, the ref had called the penalty, and he wasn't taking it back. So, there was no more to talk about. But Vernon kept going with it.

"That dude was picking on me, man. Coach, that dude *sucks*. You know the ref didn't see when he was talking trash *to me. . . .*"

He was just going on and on. I said, "You know what, Vernon? Come on to the sideline. Just come over here and sit down. Cool out."

We're still in a ball game, so I'm trying to manage my player and get back to coaching. To make matters worse, we were *losing*.

But Vernon kept going with it. "I don't like what he did. You know, man, I'm *tired* of these guys picking on me. . . ."

I mean, Vernon just kept going and going. So, I finally put my foot down and said, "Vernon, I need you to go over there and sit down. Okay? Go over there and sit down and cool out."

As soon as I turned away from him, Vernon started talking to his teammates about it. "Man, I just don't appreciate him. You see what he did, right?"

Now he was making a scene and drawing his teammates into it. But he got the flag by himself. And I'm thinking, *You know what? This is not going to work. This is unacceptable.* And so, right when he went over and sat on the bench, I can't remember exactly what he did, but he sat on the bench and started talking to his teammates about me taking him out of the game.

Well, Vernon was so pissed off after the play that I took him out of the game because he had the wrong attitude. When I took him out of the game, I told his coach. But Vernon went over to the bench and was still a disruption to the team.

I told his coach, "Find another tight end. He's done for today."

So, Vernon is sitting over on the bench, and now he gets *more* pissed off that he can't finish the game. Basically, everybody's screwing him, right? And I'm getting tired of this, you know. Now

INTRODUCTION

I'm getting angry. So, I went and spoke to the team doctors and trainers about it.

I said, "We don't need this out here. Has there ever been a guy sent to the locker room? Can I send him? Because I don't want him anywhere around this team right now. He's really hurting the team with his acting out."

At that point, everybody was watching and listening to Vernon on the sidelines instead of paying attention to the game. So, the trainer told me, "I don't think there's ever been a guy sent to the locker room. I don't think that's ever happened. But I don't think there's a rule against it. I think you can do it."

So, I said, "I want him to go to the locker room."

I went over to Vernon in the middle of him talking to his teammates to address my concerns about him being a disruption. I said, "Vernon, go to the locker room. You're done." I figured I would talk to him about *why* later.

Vernon looked at me and said, "What?"

I said it again, "Vernon, go to the locker room."

Now he's like, "What do you mean, go to the locker room?"

"Go to the locker room. You are done," I repeated. "We don't need you out here anymore."

He finally got the point and got ready to head to the locker room. Then I told him, "Get your helmet and take that with you."

Vernon started walking to the locker room with his helmet, and that's when some of his teammates started asking, "What the heck just happened?"

You know, you had some guys who were still on the field and coming in and out of the game, who weren't really paying attention to what Vernon was doing on the sideline. They didn't really understand the dispute, but that's exactly what took place.

The thing that really frustrated me was that I had been trying to coach Vernon from the beginning—while he was disrupting practice—at least every other day. There was always *somebody* getting under Vernon's skin. It got to the point when we couldn't even *practice* with Vernon. So, I started looking at Coach Nolan, and Coach Nolan was saying, "Hey, Mike, you know what? He's just young. He just has to grow up."

But I said, "We don't have *time* for him to grow up. We gotta get this team *right*. I mean, he has to do better than this."

You know, I was more concerned by Vernon's behavior than Coach Nolan was, but we were all in it together because we had to get the *team* ready for the season, and Vernon was a big part of our plans.

So, I would meet with Vernon the next morning after practice and just tell him, "Vernon, come on, man. We gotta do better than this. You got so much more to give than you're giving us right now."

He would always sit there and say, "I hear you, Coach. Yes, sir. I understand. I know."

Again, he was always respectful. *Always!* He would never be disrespectful to you, but he still wouldn't cut out the behavior of arguing and fighting with his teammates, let alone the other teams. And it was a problem.

So, when I took over the head coach position in 2009, Vernon and I *knew* that something needed to happen to really get his attention. I never knew that it would turn out the way it did, and I really didn't care at the time that it was happening. All I knew was that whatever it was going to take to make Vernon understand that I really *meant* what I was saying, we were just going to have to do it. Because I needed us to develop into a *team*, and that goal could not be held hostage by one player.

So, after the game, when I had the press conference, my hope was that something *positive* would come out of it. You know, I certainly didn't think it would get as big as it did. But the next day, that press conference was blowing up everywhere—from that evening on. I never thought any more about it. I said what I said and was ready to get back to coaching. I wanted the *message* to come across to Vernon and his teammates. We had to become a better *team* by taking our jobs and one another seriously, without all of the extra distractions. If anyone on our team is not about us coming together, including myself, then they need to be *removed* from the team.

That's how I really felt about it. I didn't care about anything else. I felt like, *This is the way I'm going to do it. And this is the only way I really know how to do it.* Right.

I've had teammates like Vernon before. I played with them. It always took something *drastic* to make them understand that there were so many other things we needed to do with the *team* that was so much bigger than their personal attitudes. I needed for all our players to understand that.

Well, after the press conference did what it did in the sports world and the media, every response I got from the other coaches was, "Thank you." I got thank-yous from the coaches *and* the players. They told me, "Thank you so much. That needed to be done. And I appreciate it. The *team* appreciates it."

That's what I got from people across the board. Now, some coaches may have been *thinking* it—the same things I said in the press conference—but they didn't say it out loud to get the response I got. I was the only one who said it in front of a microphone. And I understood that. Sometimes you're going to stand alone.

But after it took place, I sat in my office and I began to think back to my own years as a player, and how the times had changed. Because we used to have teams where we had some kind of *leadership* on the field and inside the locker room. We always had somebody who could go in there and get the attention of the other guys without the coach ever being involved.

You know, we always had somebody on the field or in the locker room who took care of that. Someone who would say, "Hey, man, look here. We're not going to have that. This is how we operate on this team."

INTRODUCTION

That was when I began to understand how the game had changed. Players don't risk as much anymore; they're less willing to walk up to another player and say anything now. Now, social media is going to get involved. Or somebody else is going to get involved with an *opinion* about what you said. Then the other players across the league get involved with their opinions. But it's nobody's business except for that *team's.* And the players on the team.

But for me, I was willing to take a *risk*—to help Vernon—that may have cost me my coaching career that day. I was just trying to help Vernon, not only for the *team* but for *himself.* I saw him being that guy who would go out to a club and he may not *leave* the club that night. You may go to the club to have a good time, and you end up snapping off at the wrong dude. And the guy pulls out something you never saw coming.

You know, some guys you just don't get into it with. You got some brothers out here who are just one word away from pulling out a gun and shooting you because they don't have anything to live for. And they don't *care.* So, I was trying to save Vernon from something *bigger* than just football. He had to get his attitude right for life in general.

Vernon was such a big, fast, and competitive guy that he was willing to go up against anybody. And I get it. Competition is a great thing. But competition—when it's *isolated*—can become a me-against-the-team thing, and that's when it's *negative* competition.

Healthy competition is when you have team players who can say, "Hey, man, look here. I'm going all-out at practice today and you need to be ready. Buckle up your stuff. I'm just giving you full warning."

That's how we used to do it as players. That's what I remember from those days. But if you come out and tell me you can't go all-out, we need to know that.

If you came up and said, "Hey, man, I can't go full speed

today. You know, my shoulder still hurts from last week," you tell me that, I'm okay with it. I'm a team player. I know guys can get hurt and sore. But when you're out there and *healthy*, and the coach says, "Hey, let's go," all right, we're going *live*. That means no holding back.

So, after the press conference blew everything out of the water with me and Vernon, that next morning, he was the first one to step into my office. I had my door closed that day. I remember I was having my prayer time when he came in because I knew it was going to be that kind of a day from what happened the day before, and how everything had gotten blown out of proportion. And I was prepared for anything that was going to happen that day.

I knew I had done the right thing, but I couldn't change some of the things that came afterward. At the end of the day, I think Vernon knew my *heart*, but I meant what I said, and if ownership had come to me and said, "Hey, you need to take that back," I would have known right then and there to move on.

I would have told myself and our owners, *You know what? You need to give this job to Joe Blow or Jimmy, then, because I'm not taking back what I said about selfish players. And I'm not saying anything different to alter my words.* I was thankful for what I said, and I was going to move on from it. But when I said it, I was only thinking about Vernon and the team, not everything that came with it. That was my attitude. So, that next morning, I was in my office, preparing myself for anything. And I came in early to have my prayer time.

When Vernon knocked at the door and I got up to answer it, he stood there in the doorway and said, "Coach, I need to talk to you."

I immediately told him, "No, I don't think you want to talk to me. I don't think you have anything to say that really warrants what happened yesterday. And I don't really think you need to talk to me right now."

You know, I had heard that Yes-sir and No-sir talk from Vernon before, but he still hadn't changed anything. So, I didn't see how one day was going to do that. I had been around Vernon for *three years* by that time.

Well, he said, "Coach, I do want to talk to you." He said, "I talked to my grandmother last night, and my grandmother said you were right. She said, 'Your coach did exactly the right thing. You were in the wrong.'"

When he told me that, I said, "Your grandmother said that? I need to meet her." I said, "I'm thankful that she said that. And I want you to understand, man, I really appreciate you being on this team. I really appreciate the talent you have. But until you turn that talent into *skill*, it's never going to be anything more."

I told him, "You got the glitter. But it's never going to be gold until you adjust your attitude."

Vernon said, "Well, Coach, first of all, I'm sorry about yesterday. That won't happen again." And he asked me, "What do I need to do? What do you want me to do to get better?"

I asked him, "What have I been telling you? You can be *great* at this game." I was still sold on his talent, but I had to be honest with him about his positive work ethic and his attitude. So, I told him, "Your blocking is exceptional. But you got hands like *rocks*. You've got to develop your hands, man. So, what do I want you to do?"

I said, "You need to start catching one hundred balls in the morning and one hundred balls after practice. You need to be catching balls in every situation until your hands are even better. And once you can block *and* catch, then you are unstoppable. If you can do that, you can be one of the most dominant tight ends in the game."

I said, "Now, after everything that we've been talking about, you're going to *exceed* all that."

Vernon heard me out that morning and looked at me. Then he started to nod his head and said, "I can do that."

The very next morning, he came and knocked on my window,

and he was already out there, catching balls in the morning. He started catching balls after practice, and that's when he began to grow *during* practice and during the *games*. And the rest is history.

Any thoughts about trading Vernon were not on my mind at the time. But if he hadn't begun to act right and hadn't changed his mentality, there would have been nothing left for us to do *but* trade him. But I wasn't thinking about trading him right then. That never even crossed my mind. I just wanted Vernon to take my message seriously.

After that, I just continued to encourage him. I would tell him, "Hey, Vernon, you know what? That's a good job, man. I like it. The development, I like seeing you do these extra things. Those are the things that you *need* to do. Now you're taking the steps of individual improvement. And when San Francisco drafted you number one, this is what they were looking for."

I said, "You keep doing that and it won't be long before you're going to be one of the leaders on this team."

Sure enough, Vernon Davis became one of our team captains. And when he started playing out of his mind on the field, I wasn't surprised by it at all. In fact, I was *hoping* for that when we got him, and I didn't know how what I did was going to work out.

You know, Vernon could have come back the next day and said, "Hey, man, you really pissed me off." And it could have gone *south* from there. But, for me, sometimes you got a spade in your hands, and you have to *play it*. Right? And I played it. So, I really prayed and hoped that it would work like it did, with Vernon becoming a leader on the team. But you've got to do different things that improve your game and your attitude to do that. Sometimes, as a coach, or even as a player, you have to take risks. Not *all* the time, but some of those risks pay off. That one with Vernon did. And I'm thankful that it paid off *hugely* for him.

As for how it went for me and my career as a head coach, there were so many spirited messages that came out of that. I had a plethora of coaches, entertainers, and leaders who called me the next day and said, "Man, thank you so much for doing that. Our young people *need* that. They need to understand that there are boundaries that we have to uphold, even if they're a star athlete or a number one draft pick. There need to be *boundaries* to how you conduct yourself in the field of play *and* in the general business of life. You know, you may have saved a person's life by demanding that they be more disciplined and team-oriented in their approach."

And so, for me, it wasn't something I did just to see how Vernon would respond to it. It was all about helping him. You know, what should I do to *help*? Because if Vernon continued like he was going, he was not only going to destroy *his* career, he would be destroying everyone else's career while he was at it, because we were not going to be an effective *team* if he remained a starter with the wrong attitude. I don't care how much talent you may have, if you're disruptive, people start thinking about you differently. You know, how is *he* or *she* going to respond this week? When you have to go out of your way like that for one player, their individual issues can start holding the *team* hostage. Then you have to think about every little thing you *do* with that player, and every little concern.

And I said to myself, "No, I'm not going to do that. I'm not going to let the elephant stay in the room. The elephant has to go. He's either going to be a team player with the rest of us or he isn't. It's as simple as that."

From there, I watched and followed Vernon's career at every opportunity. I always watched him and looked forward to his success. And I realized that Vernon was just one of those guys who had a chance to break out of the place he was in. We don't always know at the time, what we need to do to get out of a funk.

Sometimes it takes something different that makes us have an *epiphany*. You know, where you tell yourself, *Wait a minute. They don't need me. The ref threw me off the field and then coach took me out of the game. They don't even have to play with me.*

That's what I really wanted Vernon to understand, that a *team* is bigger than a *player*. And it's great to have a great player. You know, I had the great Walter Payton as my teammate. Now the league gives out an annual Walter Payton NFL Man of the Year award for team leadership, sportsmanship, and community service, where you're able to think *more* than just about yourself inside *and* outside the locker room. When you have a great player who is also a *leader* and a team *contributor*, that's when you really have something. And that's what Vernon became.

I hear he's acting and producing movies and television programs now, I'm just *excited* for him. He's another great young man I've been fortunate enough to help, and it breaks my heart that I don't have enough *time* to sit down and mentor all the young men who call me and say, "Mike, I need to talk to you, man. I'd like to hear your advice on this situation with my son." Or, "I got into this situation with my wife," and so on.

It breaks my heart that I haven't had the opportunity to spend more time with young guys like Vernon. I'm so proud of his growth, yet we're *all* still learning. When I can say or do something that can make a difference in somebody's life, it blesses me. And I'm thankful for that.

I was obedient to the voice in my heart that day. I didn't think about professionalism. I didn't think about the repercussions or what people were going to say about it. I didn't care about all of that. That back draft noise was always going to be there. But there aren't many people who are going to risk their own careers while putting it all on the line because they care so much about *you*.

In all my years of playing football, I've done a number of different things as a leader. When I played ball myself, whether it was going to the coaches and saying, "We're not practicing today. We got a teammate who's hurt, and he can't practice another day out there on the ice. We're making all this money as an organization, but we're not going out today. We're shutting it down until we get some kind of *promise* that we're going to get a practice bubble so we can practice inside, like these other teams do that we're playing against."

You know, Chicago was one of the coldest cities in the NFL, and they still had us practice outside on icy Chicago fields with no bubble or heat to protect ourselves in. So, as a team leader, I had to say something about it.

Those are the kinds of things I just thank *God* that I was able to do as a leader. And we were able to get an indoor facility in Chicago to protect us in the cold. So, when I looked at Vernon, that's where he was *at*, where he needed an *epiphany* about his life. And he had to tell himself, *Either I'm going to do this to be a leader, or I'm not.*

But I'm *tired* of hearing people talk about what they think about this or that, when their thoughts and opinions don't matter. What really matters is exactly what Vernon did by asking himself, *Do I have strong enough convictions about life to make a necessary change?* And if those convictions are strong enough for me to take action and do something about it, ask yourself, *Then what can I do?*

Vernon Davis heard my message, and he took action to make the necessary change that improved his life. And for that, I am so tremendously proud of him.

—Coach Mike Singletary

~ Coach Mike Singletary is an NFL Hall of Famer and the legendary middle linebacker from the all-time famous Chicago Bears 46-Defense. He is working on a new book of his own, *Navigating the 7 Cs of Life to the Lighthouse*, by using the steps of the seven "Cs" to get there: Courage. Consciousness, Consistency, Competence, Commitment, Confidence, and Character.

Chapter 1
Jacqueline & Otis

I'M THE OLDEST OF MY FAMILY, WITH THREE BOYS AND FOUR GIRLS. Of the three boys, it's me; Vontae, who's four years younger; and then Michael, who's eight years younger. After Vontae, my sister Veronica was born. She's a year younger than him. Then Michael came after her, before our three baby sisters, Ebony, little Jacqueline, and Christina were born. Most of the time we called Jacqueline "Jackie" for short, and with me being the oldest brother, I had to look out for all of them.

I remember Veronica as being very studious and always in her books. She was probably the smartest person in the family. She was the straight A student, always getting a 4.0. As the third child in the family, she was also in the house a lot; you know, she was a homebody. She never really partied, went outside much, or did any of that.

Then you had Michael, who was very quiet. In fact, he was super quiet, the quietest person in the family. He didn't talk much at all as a kid; he just observed things and his surroundings. After Michael was Ebony, who had a lot of opinions about things. She was not as quiet as Michael, but still quiet compared to me and Vontae. When Ebony had something on her mind,

1

she would say it loud and proud. Little Jackie was similar to Michael. She was also very quiet. But she definitely wanted to do what she wanted to do, like our mother. You couldn't tell little Jacqueline anything otherwise.

Christina was the baby of the family, and come to think of it, she was very quiet too. Hell, I guess you could say I had very quiet siblings. When Christina got older, she had a very strong relationship with my kids because she was always coming out to visit us in California.

All in all, I would say I did a pretty good job helping to raise my younger siblings. But I always received help and support from my grandmother, Adaline, and my grandfather, Lynwood. They did all the work to keep us on the straight and narrow.

My grandmother wasn't able to do that with her own kids, though. During the 1980s, many neighborhoods in Washington, DC, were overrun with drugs. My mother, Jacqueline, and a few of my aunts all struggled with drug addictions in the Petworth District of Northwest, not far from Howard University.

The 1980s and '90s were all about the crack cocaine epidemic in DC, which led to many territorial murders. You know, the effects of crack cocaine caused a lot of people not to care. They just dressed any way they wanted to and walked up and down the streets looking for that next high. You could tell who they were just by how they walked around the neighborhoods. They all acted like they weren't really there, like they were aliens, sleepwalking on earth or something. The drug addicts always looked suspicious.

However, all of those people were regular American citizens at one time. Like my mother, who was light-skinned and stood about five-nine. She was very muscular and athletically built. But she didn't play a bunch of sports and stuff like I did. My grandmother told me that my mother was a cheerleader and that's about it. Miraculously, she remained athletic and muscular even though she did a lot of drugs.

PLAYING BALL

My grandmother said my mom used to be really pretty when she was younger. She was a pretty girl, but that's all I know about her. She was a proud Leo, with a birthday on August 12. That's all I can think of concerning her youth. I think she was, like, nineteen, when she got pregnant with me. I guess she started doing drugs after that. But like I said, the drugs never really affected her body. She never looked rail thin or sick. I have no idea where she got her build from; she just had it. Maybe she got it from her biological grandfather. Even though I was darker than my mother, we still look alike. You know, I have the same general shape as my mother. I have the same shaped face. I have the same forehead. I would even venture to say that my eyes are the same as hers.

My youngest sister, Christina, is extra tall now, just like our mother. In fact, she's even taller at, like, five-eleven or maybe six feet. My grandmother Adaline is only five-five. So, again, I don't know where they got all that height from. It's a mystery to me. I have to keep guessing that my biological grandfather was tall and muscular, and that his genes were passed down to all of us from our mother.

I actually never met my mother's father, who would have been my biological grandfather, because my grandmother never married him. Instead, she married Lynwood, and he's who I grew up with as my grandfather. Lynwood was all we knew. My grandmother didn't even talk about anyone else.

That's pretty much how my life started out in DC. As I mentioned before, my mother was on crack during the heavy drug years of the 1980s and '90s. Drugs were everywhere in DC back then, and she struggled with a crack cocaine addiction like thousands of other people in the District. So, my grandmother Adaline helped raise me and my six siblings. With me being the oldest—with a different father from my younger brothers and sisters—my grandmother took me in first and raised me the

3

longest, while our younger siblings spent more time with my mom and stepfather, Otis.

My mother, Jacqueline Davis, first met Otis Willis when she was talking to a nephew of his, and she started seeing him on the side. Otis admitted that it was awkward the way he ended up with my mother after his nephew had dated her. But she kept coming to see him, so he eventually had to tell his nephew to basically move on, because he didn't want to be tied to an older woman who was already choosing an older man to be with. He said his nephew was only around eighteen at the time. Otis said he always had people coming over to his apartment to drink and party instead of going to the nightclubs. So, women were used to being around him like that.

Then he said my mother kept coming to hang out with him, and one thing led to the next, you know. When my mother got pregnant with my brother Vontae, that's when it all hit the fan. My mother continued to talk to Otis, while his nephew fell back.

Otis had just broken up with a girlfriend around that time, so when he started dealing with my mother, it was just him and her, and they ended up hanging out together a lot. My mother even got a key made to his apartment without him knowing about it. Otis didn't know she was pregnant at first either, and he felt guilty about being with her while she was still in and out with his nephew. To deal with his guilt, he told her he didn't want to be involved with her like that anymore, and she should give him his key back.

When my mother told my grandmother Adaline that Otis had basically put her out while she was pregnant with his child, she called and told him what he had done. Well, once Otis found out that my mother was pregnant, that changed everything. He told her she could come back to his apartment to stay with him. Then he had to explain it all to his nephew. Otis said his nephew didn't talk to him for, like, a year after that. He was still young, so he eventually got over it and dated girls his own age.

4

Otis stayed with my mother from that point on and ended up having six kids with her in a relationship that lasted more than thirty years of ups and downs, until my mother passed.

No matter what Otis had to go through with my mother, with her smacking him, calling the police on him, cursing him out, and a whole bunch of other stuff, he said he kept coming back because he didn't want some other man raising his kids. He wanted to be there for us the way his father was there for him and his family. He said he didn't want his kids to be calling some other man "Daddy."

I wasn't around my mother when she was running the streets, so Otis said he first met me when I was a one-year-old who was just starting to walk. He and my mother used to take me out to the park with them. I was only a baby then, so I'm sure he remembers a lot more about how things were at the time than I can. He said I had a small body with a big head that you couldn't get a turtleneck over. He said he used to play baseball with me using a miniature ball and bat, and I could really hit the ball too. I guess I had great eye and hand coordination, timing, and anticipation, even at an early age.

One time, Otis said I climbed up a tree and went so high that he was hesitant to go up after me. He said I didn't want to come back down either, because they were upset and my mother was hollering at me for climbing up so high, and I thought I was going to get a whooping when I came down. So they had to convince me that I wouldn't get in trouble once I climbed down. That's how they finally got me out of the tree.

Otis joked and said he knew I was going to reach great heights in my life after that because I wasn't scared to climb high up in that tree at such a young age. That day was like a forecasting of my life, and he was scared to climb up there to get me.

Like I said, my grandmother was the one who really raised me. I just spent a lot of weekends with my mother and Otis at their place in Southeast DC. Otis said that even then I liked to sleep in the bed with my mother and grown-ups. He said I didn't even want *him* sleeping around my mom, and he would head to the couch or sofa in the living room until I fell asleep, so he could move me out there and swap positions. I was doing that at four and five years old. When I got older, I always slept in the living room on a pullout couch in Southeast, me and Vontae.

Otis also said I used to wash my hands a lot whenever I came into the house from playing, and that I would use toilet paper for everything, including drying off my hands. So, every time I came over to their place, they were concerned about how much toilet paper I would use. I guess I picked up those habits from my grandmother. She always told me to wash my hands and she had extra toilet paper in her house—more than Otis and my mother typically had at theirs. So, they often referred to me over there as the bed space and toilet tissue bandit.

I never really felt comfortable at their house over there in Southeast DC, though. Even after my younger siblings were born, I remember I kept feeling like my mom would get up and leave us all in the middle of the night. Yeah, she actually did that to us, her *and* Otis. So, I was always anxious over there at bedtime.

I didn't know or like all of the guys over there in Southeast either. I didn't really have a crew over there like I would have around my grandmother's block when I got older. I remember I got into a mix-up with an older kid who lived near their apartment who I was afraid of. He was trying to fight me one day, so I ran to the front door of the house to get in.

This Southeast DC kid was probably, like, two or three years older than me, and dark-skinned. He was pretty rough too, you know, as far as kids go. He was what you would call a "roughneck." So, he would start with me every time he saw me coming back to the neighborhood, where he would call me "Sweetie" and throw stuff at me. Then he started chasing after me, like he was going to beat me up or something. And it seemed like he

6

was only bothering me. I don't remember him bothering anybody else.

Well, Otis saw me running and trying to get into the house to escape this kid that day. He and my brother Vontae were in the house and watched it all play out from the window, while neither one of them would let me into the house. As I beat on the door, they both looked out the window to see who was chasing me.

Otis said, "You're not running in here from him. You stay out there and fight him. You're not getting in the house."

I don't think he knew who this kid was because he probably would've said something to him directly, but he and my brother stayed inside, watching it all from the window. I think that was right before I started running around with my T-Mob crew at Truesdell, but I had to fight alone and fend for myself in Southeast.

I had no other choice but to fight the kid that day. I turned around to face him—a kid who was bigger and older than me— and I remember being mad that I had to fight him. I was mad that I couldn't just go inside the house. I was mad that I was even over there in Southeast DC to begin with; I liked being around my grandmother's neighborhood in the Northwest much better.

Well, I guess I must have turned all of that anger into hard punches because I just went off on the guy and started nailing him in his face like Mike Tyson. I don't know what I was expecting, but I don't think anyone expected me to beat him down like I did. Even Otis and Vontae were surprised. I guess they figured I was going to lose and pick up the pieces from there. But when I won the fight and sent the boy scrambling, Otis and Vontae were proud of me. They couldn't believe how badly I had whipped him. Otis even ran out of the house to pull me off the boy because I was beating him so bad. He was like three or four years older than me!

7

Otis said I was generally a good kid who didn't bother anybody. At least when I was over there in Southeast with them. He also said he had never seen me be that *mad* before, like I had turned into the Incredible Hulk or something. Vontae saw it too, so my little brother knew I had a temper after that, and that it could flare up where I could really hurt somebody. He knew he would have to stand up to people trying to bully him just like I had to do.

Ironically, after that big fight in Southeast, I never even saw that kid again. It was like he dropped off the planet. That day was a big lesson for me and for my brother. Other than this physical altercation, I was usually in a good mood. I just didn't like being over there in Southeast.

I remember their air conditioner and heating system didn't work. So, we would be cold in the winter and hot in the summer. It was so hot in their apartment, we would walk around with our shirts off all day and hop in the shower to cool off because the AC wasn't working right, and the fan would cool us off after a cold shower. We would do that and repeat the process in that apartment all day long. That's how hot we were.

Another inconvenience was that their apartment only had two bedrooms. That forced us to share a bedroom with, like, three or four kids, and I couldn't sleep all cramped up and crowded like that. So, me and Vontae would sleep out in the living room on a pullout sofa we had stretched out into a bed.

I also remember the time I was visiting them when Otis got shot. I was a little older, a teenager by then, but I still can't remember what it was all about. I just remember it was a lot of grown-up commotion out there that day. I was standing right next to Otis when he suddenly pushed me aside and into the house. Fortunately, it wasn't a life-threatening incident or bullet for him. But there was always something extra going on over there in Southeast that I didn't like—shoot-outs, fights, and all kinds of stuff.

Otis admitted to me when I was older that he and my mother used to sneak out at night when I was staying with them. Sometimes they'd be right out in front of the house. Other times they would leave me there with the other kids. In their minds, they thought that I was the oldest and I would know what to do to look after everyone. But I didn't like that *at all*, man. My grandmother never left us by ourselves. The few times that she did, she'd always tell us where she was going.

Otis told me later that he felt guilty about leaving us in the house like that, when I would call my grandmother on the phone late at night to come and get us. I mean, that was a lot of pressure on me as a kid. To make things worse, Otis got into a lot of fights with my mom, which was awkward, because most of the time, she had started it. You know, my mother was just out there. One minute she would say she loves you and curse you out the next. It was all too much for a kid to take. I didn't like being around all that negative energy.

Everything about their apartment in Southeast was out of my comfort zone, especially when my mother tried to discipline me. I don't think I had the same level of respect for my mother that I had for my grandmother. In fact, I *know* I didn't. My mother was still on drugs and walking around crazy sometimes. So, when she decided to beat me for something I did one day, I just snapped.

I yelled at the top of my lungs, "I'm never coming over here anymore! I hate being over here!"

I can't remember how my mother responded to me, but I meant it. From that moment on, I tried to stay away from her place in Southeast DC, as much as I could. Usually, I only went over there on the weekends. When I really got into sports, I didn't have a lot of free time to visit her and Otis anyway. Every part of my day was filled with something I had to do. That was when Otis started coming out to my ball games because I wasn't coming to see them or any of my brothers and sisters at their house anymore.

There was one time when I was visiting them that I got into trouble for smoking rolled-up leaves like it was weed with my friend, Jason. I was a little older by then, but not quite a teenager yet. We had the leaves rolled up in paper. Of course, all it made us do was choke. When Otis found out what we were doing, he told us not to do that again because we could poison ourselves by smoking stuff that wasn't supposed to be smoked.

Otis always had respect for me, though, and so did the other kids in their neighborhood. I didn't hang around there much, but the kids knew not to mess with me after I beat that one guy down, and that gave Vontae a lot of respect too. Everyone knew I was his older brother and, if needed, he could call me up or come get me or whatever. But Vontae never really did that. You know, we were more into sports and minding our own business, but we could still bring it if we had to.

Yeah, man, Otis respected me for everything, and he always treated me as the oldest brother and my mother's first child. So, it was kind of a big learning lesson for him to demand that I stick up for myself and show them all the way. It was, like, my responsibility of being the big brother. You know, I had to step up, and Otis knew that.

One thing I did like to do when I was over there was play football with Vontae. We would get together, find a ball, and play football around the clock. My brother was just naturally good at football, and he would follow my directions on things every time I worked out with him. He was just an *athlete*! He could run like I could, and ran sprints at Dunbar High School in track-and-field, just like I did. But Vontae was smaller than me, so he played the cornerback position.

Vontae ended up making the NFL and playing for ten years after going pro a few years right after me. Then we had our youngest brother, Michael Davis, who I felt was the best athlete in the family. Unfortunately, Michael never got to capitalize on his athletic ability because he was accused of killing a man right around the corner from my grandmother's house in the Petworth area. Michael had started going around hitting people in the back of the head with a sledgehammer. We found out later that he was a paranoid schizophrenic. That all happened around his sophomore year of high school.

I was in San Francisco when my grandmother called and gave me the news. It was *crazy* because Michael was my quarterback whenever I came home during the offseason. He'd throw me the ball and put it right on the money. He was, like, so talented. As I said, in my opinion, he was better than me and Vontae. Vontae and I were both first-round draft picks, so that tells you that Michael could probably have been a first-round pick too. And he could play any position.

His diagnosis of paranoid schizophrenia threw me off. We don't know how that happened. Maybe it could have been because my mom was using drugs all the time when she was pregnant with him. He could've had a mental imbalance, or maybe it was something else. I don't really know.

Our neighborhood high school in the Petworth area was Theodore Roosevelt, located right near Georgia Avenue. That area may not look it because of the healthy green grass and trees, but it was *rough*. Petworth was always one of the worst areas in the district. With my mother dealing with her drug issues, I used to walk up and down the street and see her and feel ashamed. Then I wondered why she never came to my football games or any of my events at high school. I didn't understand how badly drugs can mess you up, to where you don't know and don't care what's going on around you, as long as you can find your next high.

To be honest, I didn't like being around my mother when she was like that. Even though she was addicted to drugs, my grandmother always pushed me to go and stay with her on the weekends during the school year because she understood how important it was to have that mother-son relationship. In the summertime, she would have me stay with my mother for, like, a week.

Regardless of what my mother was going through, my grandmother never wavered on the importance of having me around her. But still, I hated being over there, particularly when Otis and my mother would just leave me in the house in the middle of the night to watch over all my siblings. That's when I would jump right on the phone to call my grandmother to come and pick us up.

We had to deal with that disappearing act from my mother whenever she would go looking for that next hit. Sadly, there was nothing we could do about it. My mother had a mind of her own and she would never let you know what she was up to. My grandmother could only do what she could to help her. But man, I used to get really embarrassed whenever I was at the playground seeing my mother walking up and down the street on drugs, like a homeless person. It hurt like hell because people would always talk about her. You know, she was right there in front of us.

Guys would be, like, "Yo, man, ain't that your mom?"

I would answer, "Yeah, that's her," with pain in my voice and my soul.

That's back when they used to call me "Little Duke" in my neighborhood, because my father was known as "Big Duke." I had my father's same first name too. But I wasn't a junior. I was Vernon Davis and he was Vernon Buchannan. I would say I had a very loose relationship with him. I look very similar to my dad. We're both, like, the same height at six-four and dark brown. We didn't get too much into things as far as father-and-son talks go. But he lived right around the corner from my grandmother, and anytime I saw him while walking to school, I would say, "What's up, Dad? How you doing?"

He would see me, and we'd interact with each other. I never spent the night over at his house or anything like that. I would just see him when I went to the playground or walked to school. Sometimes, he would give me a few dollars or whatever, like, a five- or a ten-dollar bill when he had it on him. But not once did he help me with homework or act like a father, outside of giving me money. He never came to a ball game or any of my events when I was older. He was a father in name only. Then I forced him to come to the NFL Draft Day in New York, when I was ready to play professional football. I'll talk about that experience later.

I did get the opportunity to meet my father's family. I met all his relatives, and they would speak to me when they saw me. I even hung out with some of my cousins on my father's side because a few of them lived right around the corner from us. I remember my father's family were all good to me. It wasn't like they tried to disown me or anything. They were always into events, with something going on. They were big on, like, bringing the family together at reunions and such. There was always something going on with them.

I remember there were a lot of males in my father's family. They didn't have many family members on drugs either. They were *workers*, a hardworking, masculine family. I had uncles on that side who owned their own companies. They would do landscaping and other manual labor jobs. I used to want to go with my father's family all the time. It was fun, you know. I used to get around my uncles, help them cut a few lawns, and make a little bit of money. What kid wouldn't want to do that?

My father had children with other women. Like, I had a brother from my dad who was only a year older than me, and two other brothers who were teenagers. Because my father lived right around the corner from us, he was never hard to find. The rest of my siblings were Otis's children.

Otis and my mother did a whole lot of experimenting with

drugs together; however, Otis didn't use drugs as much as my mother did. Man, it seemed like my mother was *always* under the influence of drugs. The few times she was sober and in her right state of mind, she was the sweetest woman you'd ever want to meet. It was like the drugs turned her into a different person.

That's why my grandmother had to step in and raise me. We had that special relationship, with me being the firstborn grandson. I never had that relationship with my mother, though. Or at least it didn't feel like it. I never really got a chance to understand who she truly was as a person, at least not in my youth. She was always compromised by the drugs. Nevertheless, I think it's important to start my memoir with a chapter about her because she's my mother, and my relationship with her was what made me so driven to succeed in life. You know, I didn't want to end up living my life the way she had hers.

My mother died on March 10, 2021, and thank God, we were in a much better place in our relationship before she passed on. Whenever I think about what I wanted to do with my life and how driven and dedicated I was, I always think about the *pain* of my mother. When pain and talent mix together, that's when you're able to persevere in your goals in life; the pain gives your talent something to feed into. It doesn't matter how smart you are or what you know; if you learn to put those two things together, to let your pain drive your talent, you can become the best at anything you do in life.

So, my mom—with all the embarrassment and hurt that she caused me in my youth—ended up giving me the drive and the fire I needed to be more and to *do* more. You know, the love that I wanted to have for her reinforced everything that I did in life, even making it to the pros to play football. The pain of dealing with my mom turned out to be my inspiration.

I didn't want to turn out to be anything like her or the people who lived around us. I wanted to be *better* than that. I wanted to *prove* something, and I felt like I had something *to* prove. So, I kept that big old chip on my shoulder ever since I was young. I owe that to my mother. Her situation created every ounce of motivation in my body to push myself forward.

I never told my mother any of this, or confided in her. I kept my distance from her until I got older because there was too much pain to deal with in my younger years. I mean, I just didn't understand what it was that I was going through with her. Once I reached the college level, that's when I started to talk about it and opened up more. That started around my sophomore year at the University of Maryland, once I was comfortable with my teammates, coaches, teachers, and surroundings. It was a situation where everyone there wanted to know who I was because I was so good at what I did on and off the football field. It was like people wanted to know, "Who is this guy?"

I began to reveal how I really felt about life. Then people started asking me a bunch of personal questions. "How do you feel about your mom? How do you feel about your dad? Who means the most to you?" The most special person in my life was always my grandmother. So, I talked about her a lot. I never mentioned my mom as being my motivation at that time because then I would have to explain her situation and her addiction to drugs. I wanted to avoid that conversation. Instead, I spoke about the person who cared for me and meant the most to me, who was my grandmother.

Once I got older, though, and then watched my mom die right in front of me, I came to appreciate her and her struggle. Now, I can say how much she meant to me. She's the reason for many of the things that I'm able to do now and all of the success that I've had in life. She was that constant example of what *not* to be that kept me pushing harder to make sure that I didn't end up that way.

It's weird, but I feel like if my mother didn't have her issues with drugs, and with me being so embarrassed by it, I don't know if I would've had the same drive and determination to succeed. I attribute a lot of that internal drive to my mother. I can't emphasize enough the embarrassment I felt; it was really there. I even saw people who were supposed to my "friends," people I grew up with, selling my mother drugs right under my nose.

I mean, what the hell was that? They had, like, no respect for me at all. You know what I mean? You can't respect a man and then turn around and sell drugs to his addicted mother. As I got older, I started to understand that my so-called friends were the same people who were killing her, little by little.

Think about it: If you're friends with somebody and you're growing up in the same neighborhood as them, and the whole time that you're out there, playing and hanging out together, and these people are selling drugs to your mom on the side. How can you consider that person to be your *friend*? Now that I'm older and wiser, I keep asking myself, "Why would somebody that I'm close to want to do that to me?"

I even had guys who were the same age as me, during our teen years and then in our twenties and even our thirties, who continued to sell drugs to my mother. I honestly don't know if she was still on drugs when she passed away a few years ago. That's still a mystery to me and the rest of my family because she always lied about taking drugs.

At the end of my football career, I understood why I was coming back to DC, and that was to be closer to my mother. In those final four years of my career, my mom grew closer to me than we had ever been in my life. We started to travel and do other things together. She even came over to the house in Maryland, which she had never done before. We went to family dinners, and she got to hang out with her grandkids. We did more in those last four years than I could ever have imagined.

Playing for the home team in Washington was a beautiful four years for me. I needed to make the transition to the next phase of my life. Then, right after I retired from Washington and professional football, my mother ended up passing away. And I was right there with her.

I remember it like it was yesterday.

I was on a movie set when I received a phone call from my grandmother, saying that my mother was in the hospital. At the time, I was executive producing another movie, *Stowaway*, starring Patrick Schwarzeneggar. When my grandmother called about my mother that day, I came rushing home to see her. When I got there, I was, like, "How is she doing?" expecting to see her alive.

They were, like, "Sorry to tell you this, Vernon, but she's already gone," though they still had her on a life support machine. So, I called in all of my family members, and we all made the decision to unplug it. It was up to me to unplug the machine right then and there in the hospital room, and I watched her take her last breath. I was at peace with it because we had gotten to spend those last few years together, and I realized that she was headed to a much better place.

We still don't know exactly what it was that took her out, but it was definitely a heart-related issue. The doctors couldn't tell us anything more than that. I just guess that all of the drugs she took finally caught up with her. You know, all of those years of doing crack with no repercussions. Your body can take only so much until it's had enough. Sadly, my mother had reached that point. It's like with me retiring from football. You just can't do it forever. Nobody can.

In those last four years with her, I would say that my mother seemed to be getting better. However, there was no telling with her because she always had a lot of tricks of deception and misdirection up her sleeve. So, there's no telling what she may have been hiding from us. She was forever manipulating what you *thought* you knew about her and what she was actually doing.

When she was not on drugs or drinking, like I said, my mother was a beautiful person. She was the most beautiful soul you could ever meet. I'm not just saying that because she was my mother. She had a loving and giving spirit. That was who she was at her core. But when she took drugs and drank heavily, you didn't know *what* you were getting from her.

That really created an awkward situation for me for most of my professional football career. I think that with all the news that circulated about my upbringing, and people asking me questions about it, everybody wanting to know what I was going through, having a mother on crack. Then it was all out in the media. There was even a special about my life on *E:60* on ESPN that included my dealings with my mother.

I did an up-close-and-personal interview, and the people who watched it knew about her already because I had become a sports celebrity, and it was one of those things, the information about my mom circulating around the league. My mother watched the special herself, and of course, she didn't like it. In fact, she got really mad and didn't want to talk about it. I told her that they were doing it because I had a story that needed to be told.

Everyone has a story to tell. With these hard, real-life stories that we live, you just hope to make other people's lives better by sharing with them what you had to go through and overcome to succeed. I tried to explain that to my mother as a teaching lesson for all of us, but she didn't want to hear it. She didn't want everything from her past to be thrown back in her face. She knew she did a lot of crazy things while taking drugs and drinking, and that they were wrong. However, for her to see her mistakes on ESPN, and then have to talk about them, was very embarrassing. It made her angry, but she did a lot of things that were not to be proud of, and eventually she had to deal with it all.

I mean, my mother was just *bad* on drugs, walking up and down the street, stealing things. She would even steal out of her own house. One year at Christmastime, she came into the house and stole the PlayStation I had just gotten as a gift. She walked down the street with it, looking to sell it to buy more drugs. I was nearly a teenager by then. I think I was, like, in sixth grade. I ran out of the house and chased my mother down the street to grab my PlayStation back from her.

I was enraged and had tears in my eyes that day. I asked my mother why she kept doing stuff like that. That's how crazy her addiction was, that she would steal her own son's Christmas present to sell on the streets. It was *crazy*! After that, we could never take our gifts over to her house. Whenever I went over there, I had to leave my valuables at my grandmother's house because my mother would try to take them to sell them for drugs. After the fact, she didn't want you talking about that kind of stuff, and she would deny that she had done it.

My mother's denial caused a lot of stress for all of us. There were long periods of time when family members wouldn't even speak to her, including my grandmother, Vontae, and all of my four sisters. We all understood what was going on with her, but we couldn't help her if she continued to deny it.

Life was *hard* for my mother, just like it was hard for me when I was growing up. Once I got older—old enough to understand it all and deal with it—I wanted to talk about my life and how it was for me. I felt an urge to understand myself and my journey in life. Every person has that right, you know.

Like, "Who am I, and why did I have to go through this?"

Talking about my life allowed me to *heal* from it, so I could forgive my mother and stop being embarrassed by her. I could never forgive her when I was younger. I wasn't in that mature mental space yet. As I grew into manhood and understood things more, I was able to form a better relationship with her and start to forgive her. That allowed my mom to become closer to me and my kids. That all happened right before she died.

Those final years became a blessing to us all, especially for my kids to get to know her better and not in the ways that I knew her.

I remember whenever I made my mother mad or did something she didn't like, she'd tell me, "I brought you into this world and I can take you out." She said that all the time. She also used to say, "It's tough to be a man," whenever I got hurt or fell down outside.

She was, like, "Get back up, boy! It's *tough* to be a man," anytime I got a bruise on my leg or an injury. She always said that: "It's *tough* to be a man!" She said it so often, I eventually learned how to be tough. Even though I was only a kid at the time, that's how my mother always wanted me to think.

And it *is* tough out there in the real world. Every person has to go through something, deal with whatever they're being challenged by. No one gets a free pass in life. Vontae had to deal with his struggles, and my brother Michael ended up dealing with what he had to deal with, and he's in a mental institution in DC to this day.

Then I have my sister, Jackie, with the same full name as my mother, who has two kids by two different men. She got strung out on heroin and hadn't even turned thirty yet. My sister Veronica had to take in one of Jackie's two kids. Veronica's a schoolteacher now, and married. She got straight A's all through school. And I'm so *proud* of her, man. She did good!

I used to feel guilty about Jackie and Michael, though, and I often wondered if I could have done more to help them. But after dealing with my mom all those years, I learned that you can lead a horse to water, but you can't force it to drink. Even if you take a person out of the negative environment they're in, if they still want to be there, they will find their way back, or link up with new people who do the same things that they're used to doing. They have to want to help *them-*

selves. There's just no getting around it. You can't make them do it. They have to *want* to do it and then follow through.

To be honest, my whole *family* had those issues. I watched what happened with my uncles, my aunts, my mom, her friends, and they were *all* on drugs and drinking alcohol back then. That's how they coped with what they had to go through in life. Alcohol and drugs became their vices and coping mechanisms. But even though I was in that negative environment, I didn't follow in their footsteps. I didn't do any of that stuff. I did nothing that would mess up my mind or my body. I stayed far away from drugs and alcohol. I wanted nothing to do with them.

But, you know, not everyone thinks the same. Everybody's built differently. Like, when people think about the money I've made, many of them just assume that I can pay my way out of the pain and struggles in life. Unfortunately, it doesn't work that way. Even when you have a lot of money, there's only so much you can do to help people, particularly if they have addiction issues. Those really are like diseases that they need to get treatment for. The money doesn't replace the dedication they need to have to get better. It's, like, a step-by-step situation that can't be rushed.

Like many of the athletes, entertainers, or other people who make good money, in the beginning, it was hard for me to say no to people because when you have it, you want to help everybody. Then, when you look back and around, you're like, "Hold up! My money's running low because I'm giving, giving, giving, and not getting anything *back.*" That's the way it always goes.

So, even though I was having fun and doing what I needed to do, while giving everything to my family that it needed, I had to watch myself and monitor my money better because I rarely got any money back in return. What happens is, dependent people start to feel like they can *always* ask you for money when they need something. It happens all the time, where they're *always*

21

asking you for something, and it becomes a vicious cycle that's hard to break.

It's like the popular saying goes, "When you get money, people think you change, but it's not really *you* who changes, *they* end up changing." Then they start asking you for money all the time when, of course, they didn't do that when you didn't have any. But once you have it, if you continue to give it to them without any return, they're going to keep asking you for it and spending it.

So, as I got older, my favorite word became *no*, even if I had it to give. I had to learn the hard way to stop enabling people and allow them to create the narrative that I owed them something just because I gave them something before.

Over the years, I had to tell my mother *no* a *lot*. She was asking me for money all of the time. But I didn't trust what she was going to do with it. My grandmother never gave my mother money either. You know, we grew up with welfare payments to help us because she couldn't keep a job. In fact, I don't know if my mother ever had a job. Maybe she had one when she was a teenager, before I was born. I never remember her having a job while I was growing up. What happened was, when my grandmother took all of us in, the government gave her checks for *all* of us.

I don't know how much the checks were for. It might have been $400 per kid or something like that. I don't really know and never asked. My mom moved into the apartment building I visited in Southeast and she kept that same apartment until the time she died. I mean, she stayed in that same property for *years*. So, my grandmother used to get the government money and pay my mother's rent, her bills, the utilities, and even, sometimes, bought the groceries. Because she was nervous that if my mother got the money, she would run out and spend it on drugs.

Reflecting back, my grandmother had so much wisdom. I

think she made sure that my mother stayed at that same apartment and never moved to a place where nobody knew her. That way, my grandmother could always check in with people who knew her and would report everything she did back to her. If my mother moved to a place where people didn't know her and what she was dealing with, they would be less likely to care or worry about her. That's not what my grandmother wanted. So, she paid to keep my mother in the same place for her own safety. Otis lived right there with her—even though they had never legally gotten married. My grandmother still looks at him like a *son* and the father of six of her grandchildren.

Otis is still around us all today, and he was *always* there for us and my mother. I remember being with him through the summer, and whenever my mom would leave at night, Otis sometimes would still be there with us. If I stayed there for a week, he would be right there with us, and I'd interact with him a lot, which was a good thing for me.

So, I continued to help out with my siblings whenever I could to make their lives easier and to keep them on point. My other sisters, Ebony and Christina, are both doing well now as adults. Christina's still living with my grandmother today, to look after her and make sure she's not alone. Only little Jackie got messed up on drugs from our next generation.

After playing professional football and his awkward retirement at the halftime of a game, my brother Vontae got into health and wellness. He even has a health and wellness clinic. His decision to set up the clinic was probably influenced by everything we went through with our mother, and then with our brother Michael and other people in the family. But Vontae's less into mental health and more into acupuncture and a lot of physical stuff that athletes use for their bodies. He has a lot of professional athletes as his clients now. They all respect and trust what he's doing.

My family has aways been secretive about the things that we've been through. But I'm not. At some point, you have to get that stuff out of your system by talking about it and dealing with it. You have to be brave enough to share the information to learn what you can from it and not keep it all bottled up inside you.

Even my grandmother never really gives you detailed information about anything. She's never talked about my mom in detail, nor any of the stuff that went on with her. At some point, we all have to understand who we are by breaking down the things that we had to go through. It's like studying a tape of a football game. If you don't look at it and discuss where you went wrong, you can end up making the same mistakes over and over again.

Chapter 2
Adaline & Lynwood

MY EARLIEST RECOLLECTION OF MY GRANDMOTHER, ADALINE, is when I used to sleep in the bed with her and my granddad, Lynwood. I slept with them until I was five years old. Then they transitioned me to a cot at the foot of their bed, where I slept until I was six or so. After that, they sent me to sleep in my aunt's room until I was eight years old. Finally, when I turned nine, I told my grandmother I wanted to sleep in my own room. That's when they gave me one, and I stayed there until I moved out of the house years later as a teenager.

With me having my own room at my grandmother's house, my aunts Pattie and Missy moved into the basement. The house wasn't all that big, just three bedrooms upstairs and a base-ment below. I had my own room, but my younger brothers and sisters had to share a room. There was a significant age differ-ence between me and my siblings; I was four or more years older than all of them. My grandparents had a lot of trust and faith in me as the oldest, and getting my own room was a reward. My grandmother's house was on the 900 block of Emerson Street, NW.

We also had a little room off the living area on the main

floor. My grandparents put bunk beds in there for Vontae and Michael to sleep on. Then they made room for my younger sisters, Veronica, Ebony, little Jackie, and Christina. Because of what I had gone through with my mother, I always felt paranoid about people leaving me in the middle of the night. Sometimes, I felt like I was going to *die* if I was left alone. I guess you could call it a deeply rooted trauma or phobia. I felt safe around my grandmother, though, and I knew that she would never leave me.

For me, it was all about the *fear* of my mom and dad not being there to comfort me when I needed it the most. Knowing that your parents are going to be there for you is important for the confidence and well-being of any child. You can feel secure just by having your parents around you, and my grandmother did just that. The same couldn't be said about my mother and stepfather, so I didn't trust them as much, and I had good reason not to.

With Vontae being the oldest kid in Southeast, he held down the fort when I wasn't there with them. Sometimes they would all be with my mom, and other times they'd be in the other room at our grandmother's house with me. I don't think they understood what was going on around them as well as I did. With me being the oldest, I took in more than my siblings. My grandmother always reminded me to look after them, but I did that naturally.

I remember my grandmother used to take me everywhere with her. I never really wanted her to go anywhere by herself because I felt like I was going to lose her. Man, I didn't even let her leave the house without me. I was just like an American Express card. I felt like somebody was going to kill her, or take her away from me. I don't know where I got those extreme ideas from as a kid, I just never trusted my grandmother going to a lot of places without me. Maybe it was the overall violent climate of DC that had me thinking that way.

So, everywhere she went, I tagged along with her, including stuff as basic as going to the grocery store. The rest of my brothers and sisters were not like that with her. It was just the nature of my particular relationship with her. Most of the time, we would leave the rest of the kids at the house with my grandfather, Lynwood.

I was so close to my grandmother that I used to lie at the foot of her bed and hold her toes. That was my favorite thing to do when I was around her. She worked as a cleaning lady for these big houses in the rich neighborhoods of Northwest DC. She never worked for a company. She was able to be her own boss, with referrals and recommendations to find new houses to clean. Her cleaning business was built and thrived solely by word of mouth. One wealthy family would tell the next one about her and she would get more work. That's how she got many of her clients.

They all treated my grandmother well too, and that extended to how they treated me. These wealthy families would let me come over and play with all their children's toys whenever my grandmother stayed over. Then they started asking her to babysit their kids. And man, I used to *love* that! I wanted to go with my grandmother all the time, so I could have full access to all their toys, bikes, and other stuff.

One of my grandmother's clients even bought her a car. I think it was, like, a Ford Escort or something. Can you believe that? That's how much they respected my grandmother and wanted to help her. I tried my best to assist her with cleaning a few times, but on most occasions, I just went with her, expecting to play with the toys and other shiny new things at those big houses.

I think my grandmother had five or six prominent residences that she cleaned. One family in particular told her that if I found any change or dollars on the floor or in their pockets while cleaning, I could have them. Of course, I loved that as well. What kid wouldn't love finding money that he could keep? I was between the ages of eight and ten back then.

So, whenever my grandmother washed their clothes, if she found anything inside their pockets, like coins, loose dollars bills, and other fun things for kids, she would give it to me. However, I never looked inside any of their clothes myself. My grandmother would always do it. One time she even found a five-dollar bill, but she gave it back to the family; she would only allow me to keep the single dollars or loose coins.

While my grandmother cleaned houses, my grandfather, Lynwood, was a maintenance man for apartment buildings. He would take out the trash, replace the light bulbs, clean up loose debris, and fix anything that needed to be taken care of. I used to go to work with him sometimes too, but not as often as I went with my grandmother. Lynwood only worked at apartment buildings on the Northwest side of DC, what we called "Uptown." They weren't really big apartment buildings, just two or four stories high, and he didn't maintain them on his own. He worked for the District in the housing authority office.

Lynwood was just like my grandmother when it came to work; he did everything he could to make an honest buck. He was, like, one of the hardest-working guys I've ever known. He inspired me by getting up every morning and doing what he had to do, even taking my grandmother's car to put gas in it for her. He used to go out at four o'clock in the morning to start the car up for her and have it warm by the time she was ready to leave in the cold winters.

What he would do was start the car with one key and lock the doors with the spare. Then he'd open the door back up with the spare key when my grandmother was ready to leave. You know, they didn't have any automatic ignitions back then, and it took a while to warm up a car in the cold.

We didn't always have the best situations as a family, but we all made it work. By the time I hit the eleventh grade in high school and had a serious girlfriend and a car, I moved out. I actually went and stayed at my girlfriend's house with her family. That was like the highlight of my life, you know, being able to wake up every morning in the arms of the girl I loved and drive to school with her. However, it was a little awkward and uncomfortable at times when I'd walk into the hallway to the bathroom in the night without my shirt on, trying to avoid her parents seeing me. So, I would sneak around the house quietly, not making any extra noise, especially when I got hungry late at night. I didn't want them thinking that I was a hungry bear in the kitchen. But sometimes I felt like I *was* a hungry bear.

It's funny when I think about my grandmother raising me and then going on to become a professional football player. I say that because she never even watched the games. She'd tape some of them and then ask me about them after the games were over. Then I would call her after the game and tell her, "Momma, I'm okay." That's when she would go back and watch them all so she and my grandfather could get the details.

Of course, she always hoped that I didn't get hurt. In fact, she never wanted me to play football because of the injuries. That's why she never watched me play in high school, at the University of Maryland, or in the NFL. My grandmother would rather have me playing basketball, but football became my bread and butter.

Because she was so leery about the physical contact of football, I didn't play on an organized team until the eighth grade. She just didn't want me to get hurt. Her main priority was taking care of her grandkids and making sure they didn't get hurt. Her love was so strong that it would mess her up to see me get injured.

She was okay with the sport of basketball, though. So, I played basketball until football took over in my high school years. Again, my grandmother was so busy raising all of us kids and keeping her house in order, she never came to see any of my basketball games, or my track meets either.

To be honest, I didn't need outside support like that. I had a lot of self-motivation and determination already. I always managed to push myself to succeed. When you grow up in the heart of Northwest DC, you learn to get it how you can and do what you have to do to get it. It doesn't matter who supports you. For me, it was just about having fun and playing sports. The lack of support from my family and the games did run through my mind a few times, but I didn't think about it to the point where it bothered me.

With the team sports that I participated in, my grandmother would sign me up and drop me off at practice, but she never stayed to watch me. That didn't mean she didn't support me. She had a bunch of other things to do and other family members to look after. She was always there for me when I needed her, though, and of course, she attended all of my graduations and other important events. She was always in my corner with my bigger decisions.

Even though she didn't go to any of my games, my grandmother was very excited when I got a scholarship to attend the University of Maryland. She was happy for me and very proud that I was living out her lessons and doing everything that she had taught me. She even helped me move into my freshman dorm. She was just *relieved* because she had so much heartache when it came to dealing with her own children, like my mother being hooked on drugs.

Outside of my interest in sports, I think my grandparents raised us to be great stand-up kids, and to always do our best in life. They taught us a lot of lessons that were really valuable. Our grandmother wanted us to be kind, to treat people well, and to do the right thing in general. She was the kind of woman who was loved by people in the community. And she didn't stick her nose in everyone's business or anything like that. It was her attitude that they liked, her realness. They all loved her work ethic and the way she raised all seven of us grandkids. That was just the way she was. She was always giving and hard at work.

I'll tell you what, though, we tore her house apart, so my grandmother stopped letting people come over. It was so messed up and dirty inside, we even had a wall heading down into the basement that we used to write and draw on. I mean, the *whole wall* was messed up. We had roaches in the house too, so I wasn't thinking of inviting anyone inside either.

I remember one time I had a girl over in the kitchen. We were sitting at the kitchen table, and every time roaches ran out on the table, I would swat them away with my hand. The girl never saw them because I was anticipating the roaches running out and I caught them before she saw them. From that point on, I kept the girls in the living room. I never took them into the kitchen anymore; there were too many roaches in there.

The inside of the house may have been messy, but my grandparents kept the outside up to par. We had old-school air conditioners hanging out of the windows like a lot of other houses on the block. My grandmother wasn't the kind of woman on block patrol, who would reprimand people out in the streets. She kept to herself and would only speak up when she had to.

Grandmother Adaline was experienced in putting in the work necessary for her kids and family, a lesson for everyone to do their best, even if the results were not what we expected. We all have to understand that just because you give children your love, teach them the right things, and bring them up the right way, that doesn't necessarily mean everything is going to end up perfectly for them because everyone has their own minds and situations. When kids reach a certain age, they're going to do what they're going to do.

What I believe happened with us grandkids is that we decided to go the way my grandmother wanted. Maybe not *all* of us, but some of us did. We just decided to do the right things, the ones she had hoped for. She felt really good about that. I'm quite sure it felt good for her, with me being the firstborn and going above and beyond what most people expected from me. I did something legendary that doesn't happen for a lot of people in the District. I had a chance to do something special, to show my grandmother what I could really *be* in life.

But before I had sunshine, I had rain. I got into a lot of trouble in my adolescent years, with bad experiences, like getting arrested, which happened before I entered the seventh grade. Once I learned my lesson, though, I changed my whole life and my way of thinking. It was like I went from being the most notorious guy out on the streets to the most righteous man in the church. That's how drastic a change I made at a young age.

At one point, I did everything you would tell a kid *not* to do. I smoked. I was having sex at an early age. I got arrested *twice*. I was on probation. I was drinking alcohol. I mean, I did everything I could to mess up my life, all during my fifth and sixth grade years of school. That was when all of my troubles popped up. I was just hanging out in the streets all day, with no structure or curfew. I still had to be in the house by a certain time, but sometimes my grandmother would let me stay out until two o'clock in the morning. But you know, it was the summertime, and I was right out in front of the house or right down the street. So, I guess my grandmother just trusted me to do the right thing while I was outside, no matter what time it was.

I stopped going with my grandmother to the houses she cleaned. Once you start doing the wrong shit, you don't want to be around the right stuff anymore. So, everything you can think of that was *wrong*, that's what I tried to do. Like going into apartment buildings and spraying the fire extinguishers, which make the air all smoky. Then we started knocking on people's doors and running away before they could walk out. In the wintertime, we would roll up snowballs with rocks in them and throw them at buses and cars. Sometimes we played this game with the police called "getting chased." What we did was throw the snowballs with rocks in them at police cars as they drove up the street, just so we could get chased by them.

The crazy part about it was that we never got *caught*. Or maybe the police didn't really want to catch us for a juvenile offense like that. Maybe they understood that we were just bored kids looking for something to get into. When we started stealing from people's houses and trespassing on their property, that was when I *did* get caught.

We also started stealing bikes and family dogs, and those were more serious offenses. We never got arrested for anything we did in the Black neighborhoods that were closer to Georgia Avenue, though. I guess where we lived was not as much of a priority. But when we went into the white neighborhoods up 16th Street, and traveled out to Maryland, that's when we got arrested.

My luck ran out the first time when I finally got myself arrested off of 16th Street, NW. That was when I got arrested for stealing bikes up there. We broke into a family garage and stole these bikes before getting cornered by the police on our way back home to Georgia Avenue. At that time, the popular bikes in DC were those Canyon mountain bikes and Cannondale and Panasonic racing bikes. Some of them were black and blue, and that's what we were after that day.

I really felt like I had let my grandmother down in a big way with the things I got into. I mean, I knew what she was trying to do with us grandkids. We could all feel the love that she was giving us, and I let her down badly. I remember when I walked out of the holding cell and saw my grandmother; she just looked at me and was *pissed*. I can't recall what she said, I just remember the look of disappointment written all over her face. As they say, a picture is worth a thousand words.

When we got home, my grandfather Lynwood was like, "You know better than that. With all your grandmother does for you, you gon' go out there and do something like *that?* You need to be *ashamed* of yourself! Now get up to your room before I whoop your ass!"

Now, I didn't get away with things without getting some well-deserved whoopings. No, sir. I used to get torn up. Lynwood used to *stay* putting the belt on me. But I had it coming. I was into a lot of bad stuff and ended up with a felony. Luckily, I was only in jail for a day before my grandparents came and got me out.

That first arrest was a misdemeanor, but the second one, which I caught out in Maryland, was a felony. That was when we got snagged trying to steal dogs. We were out in the Prince George's County area, right outside of DC, and broke into a house to steal this expensive miniature dog. It was a puppy, but I can't remember what breed it was. All I remember is that it was a miniature and very expensive. We were planning to take dogs back to the District and sell them there.

That second arrest changed everything for me. I told myself, "Man, I can't keep hurting my grandmother like this." I remember walking into the house and telling her, "Momma, I think I'm going to pull back from my friends because I don't want to keep getting into trouble. I don't want to keep hurting you."

She said, "Okay, but let me tell you something. Just because you're not hanging with them anymore doesn't mean you have to turn your back on them, because you never know when you'll need them."

That's what she told me. That was the last straw for me, man. I went the straight and narrow after that. As I said, the thing that made me change was not wanting to hurt my grandmother anymore. I also wanted to be successful in life. So, I got back into playing basketball and focused on sports. But I still wasn't play-

ing football yet. We always played basketball in our neighborhood as soon as we felt we could shoot a ball through a basket.

I felt that I could change things for the better if I really focused. I told my grandmother when I was still young, "Momma,
every penny you gave me, I'm gonna pay you back. One day, I'm
going to give you a lot of money." I used to tell her that all the
time: "Momma, I'm going to give you a lot of money one day."
That's what I called her. I called my grandmother "Momma,"
and my mom was "Ma."

Back then, I never had any money. We were still living on welfare, and I remember in my teenage years, my girlfriend,
Janel—my children's mother—helped me out a lot. She even
helped me move into the dorm with my grandmother at the
University of Maryland. I had my own car by then, and it wasn't
too much for us to move my clothes and things into the dorm.

When it was time for me to leave school early at Maryland and
go pro, my grandmother really didn't understand what was
going on. My grandparents weren't aware of how much *money*
professional athletes were making in sports. So, I sat both of
them down, Adaline and Lynwood, and I looked into their eyes
and said, "Momma, I'm going to leave school early from Maryland as a junior. I got a chance to make a lot of money in professional football."

They looked at me and said, "Grandson, why would you want
to do that?"

You know, a college education is what we all think about when
you get a scholarship to go off to school. Right? But once I became recognized as one of the premier tight ends in the college
game, the National Football League (NFL) started ranking me
as a top ten pick in the 2006 NFL Draft, which was *huge*. But my
grandparents didn't know that. An NFL salary was all new to
them.

So, I repeated myself: "Daddy, I can make a lot of money by

going pro and taking care of y'all. I can change the dynamic of the whole family. I mean, I'm really about to make a lot of *money*," I told them. "I have a real high draft grade as one of the top ten players in all of college football."

Imagine telling hardworking, blue-collar Black people that you're about to make *millions* of dollars playing professional football. I mean, they were looking at me like I was *crazy*. It was just too far out there for them to comprehend. To this day, I still don't think they *believed* what I was telling them. My grandparents continued to stare at me and didn't get it. By that time, I had gotten really far in sports by working hard and making great decisions, so they trusted me and accepted my judgment on it.

My grandmother finally nodded and said, "Well, whatever decision you decide to make, we'll support it. We'll just pray about it."

She always told me that before making a big decision. It didn't matter what it was, my grandmother would always say, "Let's just pray about it." That's exactly what we did before I left the University of Maryland after my junior year.

It was just one of those unbelievable things. It wasn't every day that a young football player was being drafted out of Washington, DC, after growing up the way I had. We had Byron Leftwich, Brian Westbrooks, Josh Cribbs, *me*, and a few other guys. DC was never a football hotbed like Florida, Texas, California, Georgia, Alabama, South Carolina, Pennsylvania, Ohio, or Michigan.

There just weren't a lot of people in the District who got a chance to experience being drafted to the pros in football. If my own son came to me and told me he was leaving school to play ball for a living, I would've looked at him like he was crazy too. I'm sure I'd say something like, "What are you talking about? How is that going to work? How do you plan on that happening?"

PLAYING BALL

I may as well have been speaking a foreign language to my grandparents that day. They really didn't understand what I was talking about. But they soon found out because the NFL invited six guys up to Manhattan, in New York, to the Radio City Music Hall for Draft Day, including me. At that time, back in 2006, only the top few college guys were invited, so we were like the cream of the crop. I ended up nearly taking my whole family.

I took my grandmother and grandfather, of course. I also brought along my brother Vontae; my girlfriend, Janel; I had a business manager who came; my aunt Sharon and aunt Missy; and my father, Vernon Buchannan, aka Big Duke, came along too. Imagine that. My father actually came with us, all squeezed into a black cargo van. We didn't have the money to pay for train or plane tickets for all of us. Somehow, I was able to convince my grandmother to go with us. And man, it was *great* to have her there.

That NFL Draft in New York City was one of the best days of our *lives*! We had never experienced anything like that. None of us! My grandmother was overwhelmed with joy, and so was my grandfather. It was a great day for *all* of us. It was like the best gift you could ever give someone to celebrate because after you get drafted, that moment changes everything.

My draft night also inspired my brother Vontae to get serious about what he wanted to do with football. I had already been preparing him for the game and working out with him, showing him the ropes and things. Eventually, it paid off because Vontae got drafted in the first round by the Miami Dolphins a few years later, and he went on to play in the NFL for ten years. He also made history as the first NFL player to retire at halftime.

Vontae was a hell of an athlete coming out of DC himself. He ran the sprints in track at Dunbar, just like I did. I feel like I had a lot to do with that by pulling my brother along with me for early morning workouts and everything else I did with him. He admitted that he was glad I decided to pull him along for my workouts too. But again, Vontae was already athletic; I just wanted to get his work ethic up. Because you can be a natural athlete with terrible work habits, and that ends up wasting your gifts. A lot of those guys with bad work ethics in high school don't go pro because it gets harder to compete at every level.

But let me tell you, when NFL Commissioner Roger Goodell called my name for the San Francisco 49ers, I was on cloud nine. I stood up to go shake hands with him and I don't remember anything else. What I do recall is the crowd yelling and me crying, while everything seemed to be moving in slow motion. It was just *crazy.*

As far as me moving out to San Francisco to play for the team, my grandparents didn't respond to that. They were just happy for me and wished me well, while praying about everything. But even after I turned pro, my grandmother wouldn't watch a football game live for fear of me getting hurt. She would always wait until after the game was over before watching it.

Lynwood watched the games, though. It really didn't matter, though, because I would call home after every game and give them the rundown on everything anyway. Whenever I had an *excellent* game, that's when they would let *me* know.

My grandfather would say, "Good game, young man."

Then my grandmother would chime in, "You did really good. You showed your *tail,* didn't you?" That's what she would say.

Once San Francisco drafted me, I had to fly out there to meet the owners and the whole organization, the coaching staff, my teammates, and get acclimated to the facilities. I stayed out there for three or four days and then flew back to DC to start preparing myself for the move to the Bay Area and the training camp for my first season.

With the money I was in line to earn from playing football, I let my grandmother meet with anyone that I planned to invest my money with. My grandparents didn't know anything about investing money, but they had wisdom when it came to trusting and understanding different *people*. My grandmother basically told me, "Just make sure you pay attention and keep your eyes on everything" concerning my money and my professional football career.

You better *believe* my grandmother was quite upset when I ended up in a very public respect-the-game dispute with San Fransisco 49ers head coach Mike Singletary during my third year in the league. I wouldn't really say she disagreed with him, but like a lot of other people, she was pissed that he went on TV and humiliated me like that to everyone. She felt, like a lot of other people, that Coach Singletary could have handled his issues with me privately instead of in front of the cameras the way he did.

She didn't feel like I deserved to be talked about on national TV that way. My grandfather didn't like it either. But years later, they both agreed that the embarrassing event turned out to be *good* for me. My grandmother said she understood how the coach felt about it, and how you need to have more respect for your teammates by not doing things that hurt them. So, she got over it and was okay with it because it helped me to learn something valuable. It also helped me to become a better person, and a better player through the principles of old-school, tough love.

In the aftermath of the big, televised dispute, everyone could see how I changed my game and my team approach. It was a change for the better that happened right away, like in the very next *game*. My demeanor about *everything* changed after that. I got much better at my tight end position too, and the difference was very noticeable.

You could tell that I was getting myself prepared to be a better person and a better leader. Really, I had no choice but to become a team leader after that incident with the coach. I figured I could stand tall and become the team leader that he wanted me to be, or I could duck, hide, and try to run from it. But I wasn't going to do that. You know, iron sharpens iron. So, I stood up and became a better man and a better teammate.

The way I thought about it, I just wanted to get my act together because at the end of the day, I still needed to learn how to channel my emotions. I still had a lot going on in my life, and I was coming from a place that hadn't really prepared me for the world of professional sports in which I found myself. I learned how to channel my emotions better *on* the football field and *off* of it, while doing the right things to become a leader.

That leadership lesson was learned years before we lost the Super Bowl to Baltimore with Jim Harbaugh as our head coach. My grandmother talked a lot about that game.

She was, like, "Y'all *had* that game! I don't know what the play calling was, I just wanted you to *win* that game so bad. I wanted that game *bad* for you."

She was really into that San Francisco/Baltimore Super Bowl, and I'm talking about *the game.* She was explaining how we threw the ball on passing routes and everything. That really took me by surprise. But the Super Bowl is definitely the next level of sports, and my grandmother had obviously gotten into it.

Many people thought I should have at least gotten one pass down there in the Red Zone at the end of the game instead of the ball going to Michael Crabtree every play. The coaching staff figured we would win with that game strategy. They just couldn't imagine Baltimore's defense being able to stop Crabtree every time, but they did. And it was just *nuts*, man. We were that *close.*

Lynwood was excited about the game too. He said, "It was all kinds of crazy calls in that game. And I don't know how the lights went out on the stadium, but y'all boys came to *play.*" He added, "Y'all did well, you just couldn't get it done. You couldn't get that *one* touchdown. But it'll come back again. You'll be back there. Watch."

He was that confident about my Super Bowl chances. Sure enough, he was right. I *did* go back, but not with the 49ers. I ended up going back to the Super Bowl with Peyton Manning and the Denver Broncos a few years later, after being traded.

In Denver, we ended up winning the Super Bowl against Cam Newton and the Carolina Panthers. My grandparents *loved it!* They were so happy for me. My grandmother said that all the hard work I had put in was for that one moment.

She said, "It doesn't really matter where you had to go, where you got the ring, or where you played the Super Bowl, all that matters is that you put in the work, you *deserved* it, and you *earned* it."

She didn't watch the Broncos Super Bowl the way she watched me in San Francisco, though. I guess she couldn't accept the fact that we could *lose* again. So, for that one, which we ended up winning, she sat around the TV and listened to what the family had to say. You know what I mean? She was *ear*-watching more than *eye*-watching.

I only played about three months with the Denver Broncos; then I was a free agent and available to play anywhere I wanted to on a new team. So, I ended up heading back home to play for Washington. My grandmother was really happy about that, and so was everyone else in the family, including old friends in DC and guys who went to Maryland with me.

My grandmother said, "You're returning home, and I'm glad you'll be close enough to come see me more."

I had always returned home to see my grandmother and family in DC during the offseason with San Fransisco, but while playing for Washington, I could see her every *week* if I wanted to. That's when I was able to get close to my mother as well. I didn't talk about that too much with my grandmother, but she said she saw it. She saw the things that my mother and I were doing together when I returned home to Washington. By that time, my grandfather was getting closer to dementia. Lynwood wasn't all the way there in 2019. Sadly, he didn't have much to say anymore.

When I retired a year later, in 2020, my grandmother said she had hoped I would have retired *years* ago. She said it didn't affect her or anyone else in the family, and it was a decision I had to make for myself. She was happy when I finally did it, though. I was happy that I had won a Super Bowl first, and then I got a chance to play for the home team for a few years in Washington. That was like icing on the cake. I just wished we could have had a few good seasons while I was there.

When I decided to get involved in acting, music, and filmmaking for my next career move, my grandmother was excited about that as well. She said she believed I could do anything I put my mind to.

"Vernon, you've proved everybody wrong, time and time again," she told me. "And you've showed everybody that you're always gonna do the unexpected, so we never know what's coming next."

Unlike football, where you don't know what's going to happen from play to play, with injuries and whatnot, my grandmother watched all of my movies because she knows that we're just acting. And she *loves it*. She gets all into it, like she's watching Denzel Washington or something. Of course I'm not Denzel Washington, but that's how excited my grandmother gets about the movies I'm in.

She encourages me by saying, "You did *good*! You're getting better and better at acting. You're doing really well. That movie was so *good*." Then she'll ask me about my next film premiere.

I think *A Message from Brianna*, which I did with Asia'h Epperson, may be my grandmother's favorite. She really liked the family horror story in that one. She also liked *A Day to Die*, which I did with Bruce Willis, Just Leon, Kevin Dillon, and a bunch of other actors. She thought that one was pretty good too, a big action movie.

Now that she knows I'm writing a book about my life, she says she'll support that and anything else I decide to do. She's just so *proud* of her firstborn grandson, man. It really makes me feel *good* that I've given her a great deal of *joy* in her heart. It really does.

On the flip side, one of the things that caught my grandmother off guard was my baby brother, Michael. Like I said, he could have been a standout football player and athlete in the District, like me and Vontae, but when he developed paranoid schizophrenia, he did some things that came from out of nowhere. My grandmother said she was confused by them.

As I mentioned earlier, at the age of nineteen, my brother was accused of killing an older man with a hammer. Michael was then charged with first-degree murder. He was also accused of attacking several other people with a hammer, not far from my grandmother's house in Northwest DC.

To this day, my grandmother doesn't think Michael committed those horrible crimes. She thinks he was set up. With the mental condition that he developed, and the people that he was hanging around with in the streets at the time, my grandmother figured that someone could have taken advantage of it. Someone else could have done the hammer crimes and blamed them on my brother.

Because of his condition, he was declared incompetent to stand trial in court and couldn't even stand up to defend himself. So, we may never know the truth. My brother has been held in that same mental institution in Washington, DC, ever since. That happened back in the spring of 2012. His situation has caused us all a lot of stress and pain. But we all came to understand that his condition could have been there from birth, with all of the drugs my mother was taking when she had him.

Of course, my grandparents were devastated by what happened and they were sad for Michael. They also felt a deep sadness for the victim and his family. In retrospect, it was one of those tragic events that just leaves you speechless. Reflecting back, they didn't have too many words to say besides, "Let's pray." They were truly at a loss for words, but somehow they managed to get through it and keep on living and helping their other grandchildren.

Chapter 3
Truesdell & Paul

I WENT TO GRADE SCHOOL IN THE PETWORTH NEIGHBORHOOD AT Truesdell Elementary, which starts at the kindergarten level. The first memories I have of Truesdell are probably from when I was in the first grade. I remember going there and feeling afraid because it was my first time attending a real school. I did pre-K at this other place called Head Start and kindergarten at Truesdell. But moving up to the first grade was the real deal for me, and I don't think I was really comfortable with school yet. I still wanted to be at home with Adaline, my grandmother.

My grandmother told me that because my birthday was in January, I had to wait to attend first grade the next school year. So, I may have been seven years old already. I'm not quite sure, but my age was probably a little different from the other kids in class with me. I do remember, though, my grandmother said I was goofing off too much and I should repeat my first school year. She didn't think it was productive for me not to get the lessons I needed to advance to the next grade. So, by the time I made it to fifth grade to graduate from middle school and move on to junior high at Paul, I was probably a little older than the other kids.

My grandmother said it all paid off for me in the end. She just didn't want the school pushing me ahead if I was still lacking what I needed to complete each grade successfully. She was my grandmother, who I absolutely adored and honored in my world, so what she said *goes*. If she thought I wasn't ready for the next grade, I wasn't ready. No arguments were needed.

However, it's hard to recall everyday things from your grade school years. You have so many of them, you know. You usually only remember the big events and the general things that you did. I loved going to recess and playing outdoors with my classmates. Man, I always wanted to go out for recess. Who didn't? That was my favorite part of going to school.

Recently, the old school building in which we first attended Truesdell was remodeled. It's a new building altogether now, so it doesn't look the same as it did in the late 1980s, when I went there, but it's still in the same location, four blocks away from my grandmother's house in Northwest DC.

It was a majority Black school back then, but we had a few Hispanics there too. There are probably more Hispanics going there now, and maybe more white kids because the neighborhood has changed so much. These days, a lot of new people are moving into DC. The city is really blossoming, becoming a lot more multicultural and international too, with a lot of people settling in DC from other countries.

I remember my favorite subject in school was spelling. I even participated in a spelling bee one year. I mean, I always liked to spell. It was fun and individually challenging for me. When I got older, my favorite subject became science. I got all into the life of plants and roots and trees, sunlight and seeds, growing plants, and all that kind of stuff.

In science class, we got to experiment with things. I loved that too. Most of us kids loved going to and participating in the annual science fairs. I mean, science was *big*, man, from elementary school all the way up until junior high.

I loved everything about science. I got to create a volcano in an experiment, then we did a lightbulb experiment and learned all about electricity. Man, everybody wanted to do the lightbulb and electricity experiment. So, here's a shout-out to Thomas Edison for coinventing the lightbulb. I think I did that science fair experiment in the sixth grade and the volcano experiment during the seventh, which was actually after my middle school years.

There was a period where I didn't like my teachers, though, especially our main disciplinarian. Mr. Robinson, a stocky Black man with a bald head and a beard, who had special duties to keep kids in order. He was a regular teacher in the school, and I wouldn't necessarily say that he was a tough man; he was just the kind of guy who always made sure everyone was on the up-and-up. He was no-nonsense and he made certain that everybody did what they were supposed to do. He also kept us moving in the hallways.

He would see you acting up and he would be, like, "All right, Mr. Davis. I'm watching you."

That's what he would say. He called everybody out by name, to make sure that *you* knew that *he* knew who you were. And he knew our whole *crew*, so he would call all of us out in the hallway. Because the teachers were so good at breaking us down on their jobs, I had a problem with Mr. Robinson, the principal, and several others at school. If I was constantly causing trouble they had to discipline me for, why would I like any of them? That's what you do when you're a misguided kid. You dislike anyone who doesn't allow you to act up.

I liked my physical education teachers, though, because I always liked playing sports during gym. That was obvious, right? I even signed up to be a tumbler in fifth grade because I could flip, and I liked being around the cheerleaders. Our colors were blue and gold, like the Los Angeles Rams.

Like any other school in a tough neighborhood, Truesdell had a few bullies who went out of their way to make things hard for the other kids. I remember this one kid named Chris who bullied me. That was back in third grade. He was older than me by about a year. Unfortunately, we all had to deal with him until he graduated.

Chris bullied me relentlessly. He took something from me every time he saw me. Man, I used to hate that. One time he took my money. The next, he took my lunch. After a while, I just got sick and tired of it. So, after about six or seven times of him taking stuff from me, I just ripped him one and went off. I started punching him in his face, like four times, hitting so hard that he took off running. The weird thing is, after that, the dude became one of my best friends. I mean, I still had to see him at school every day. After I ripped him one, he would just stop and look at me. Every time I walked by him, he'd look at me, and he wouldn't say anything. He would just stand there like a statue. But he definitely wouldn't try me anymore. After a while—I don't remember how our conversations started—but we just connected and started hanging out, playing basketball together and running around.

In fact, playing basketball is how our new relationship started. I was out on the court one day, and Chris just walked up and started hooping with me. That's what kicked off our new friendship. I don't remember anything specific that he said to me; it was just us being active together. I hung out with that dude all the way up until the ninth grade, when I went to high school at Dunbar.

I also had another best friend when I went to Truesdell, a kid we called JuJu. His real name was Kevin Mack, and he was just *cool*, man. We clicked and were best friends all the way up until seventh grade. Me and JuJu did a lot of stuff together. We

48

even taught ourselves how to do backflips, flips off the monkey bars at the playground, and flips off gates and fences. We did all kinds of acrobatic stuff, like we were making videos for YouTube or something.

Me and JuJu were, like, the only daredevils who could do all those extra tricks. People used to watch us a lot. He was fast, too, a little faster than I was back then. We used to race each other all the time, and we spent a lot of time together, hanging out. I remember one of his favorite games was "keep away," with tennis balls and footballs at recess. Another game we used to play was called "throwback," where nobody could catch JuJu. It was, like, once he got the ball in his hands, he was gone until he got tired or until he let you catch him.

JuJu wasn't a pretty boy or anything like that, but he always had long hair and braids and could get attention from a lot of girls. He knew how to talk to them and how to make them laugh, and the girls liked him.

I remember we used to play "Freaky Friday" at school, where you chased a girl and touched her, and the girls had to run from us. With me and JuJu being some of the fastest guys at school, you know we were good at that. Chasing down girls was easy. So, that was big fun.

In fourth grade, a girl named Tiffany Barnes became the first love of my life. I remember her like it was yesterday. I loved that girl, man. She was my everything, and the first person I fell in love with. She was light-skinned and pretty, with an amazing personality. She was medium height with dark hair, dark eyes, and a nice frame. When the fifth grade school year came around, she was my official girlfriend.

Tiffany was my girlfriend in the fifth *and* the sixth grades. During the summer break after sixth grade, we broke up, and my boy JuJu started talking to her. Of course, I had a bad taste in my mouth about that. Why did he have to choose her out of all the other girls in school, you know? We even got into a fight over that. And you know what happened? JuJu slapped me in my face and ran because he knew I couldn't catch him.

I got so angry that I found a log from an old, medium-sized tree, and I picked it up and launched it in the air at him. Man, that damn thing came down and smacked JuJu right on the top of his head. He fell down fast and hard, just like one of those cartoon characters you see on TV.

JuJu climbed back up and started jumping up and down, like, "Got damn, man! Damn!"

It was unbelievably funny, so I broke out and started laughing. Then I started running away from him when he got mad. I mean, I didn't expect that log to hit him like that. But I felt like my best friend should've never done that to me. He knew how I felt about Tiffany. Then she tried to get back with me in junior high school at Paul, but I kept giving her the cold shoulder. I just didn't want to hear it.

I felt like, *How in the world could you talk to my best friend and flirt with him like that?* She knew we were best friends. She even caused a fight between us. So, it was on to the next one for me. Over time, you get over it. But I still follow Tiffany Barnes on Instagram years later as a grown man. I will never forget the time I shared with her as my first serious girlfriend in DC.

I even remember the first party she had that I went to. It was at Chuck E. Cheese for her birthday. She was my little girlfriend, so of course I was there with special attention. I just wanted to be around her as much as I could. I gave her a gift for her birthday too, a pair of new sneakers with money my grandmother had given me. I can't remember what kind of sneakers I bought her. She was happy with them, though. That was during the time when people would kill you over a pair of Michael Jordans. But I know I didn't buy her any of those. Jordans were expensive, even in kids' sizes. Nevertheless, I remember Tiffany gave me a big hug for that birthday gift. We weren't into kissing and all that stuff yet. We were still young with puppy love, and satisfied with that.

Outside of my young love interest, with my guys, JuJu and Chris, we formed this neighborhood school group we called T-Mob, standing for Truesdell. Yeah, we had a little gang going on at school. T-Mob was like the Truesdell area boys forming a young mafia. You know what I mean? It was all about being from Truesdell. That's where we hung out, so we just called it a mob. We had an alliance to hang out together. And anybody in our group, we protected.

It was me, JuJu, Chris, BJ, Ronald, Big Donald, Davon, and more guys. There was, like, *twenty* of us in the T-Mob crew, all going to Truesdell together. We would just meet up around school and do our thing, getting into trouble and what-not. Everybody didn't do the same kind of crimes together, whether it was a school day or during the weekend.

Our crew wasn't all about getting into trouble, though; we had fun playing sports too. We played basketball against any and everybody, whether they were from our community or from another neighborhood. You know, the different crews in each neighborhood all knew one another, including the Ninth Street guys and the guys on Seventh Street. Everyone in the community had their own little set, depending on what neighborhood you lived in. Because we all knew one another, it wasn't like we were fighting or anything like that. Everyone just played sports against one another, whether it was basketball, football, or even bike racing.

The initiation to get into T-Mob was *crazy*, too. One of my friends got sprayed with mace. I had to walk up to this random guy and punch him in the face. That's the crazy kind of stuff we had one another doing. They gave me my assignment: "Go punch that guy in the face."

To give me a reason for doing it, my crew told me to lie and say that he tried to assault my little sister, but of course, he hadn't. I went and punched this unknown kid in the face anyway because it was part of my duty, to show my crew that I was seriously down for whatever.

This guy was a little bigger and a bit older than me, but I punched him hard in the face, and he ran away. We were right around the Truesdell schoolyard, where we hung out every day. Most of the time, we were just hanging out in our neighborhood. And man, I got a lot of respect on the streets after I did that. I felt comfortable with the attention that it got me too, because it was our own 'hood in the Northwest, where I knew a bunch of people.

Well, as it turned out, because the guy who I punched in the face went to school with us, he went right to the principal's office and told on me, which got me suspended. I couldn't even lie about it because everybody was out there and saw. So, I got suspended for three days for fighting.

If you were really bad in school, what they would do is take you out of your classroom and stick you in Mr. Robinson's office with your desk. That's what actually happened with me. It was straight confinement and all schoolwork in there. You couldn't even go to any activities. In fact, I was in the principal's office quite a few times for acting up, in school and out. But they never let you stop learning at Truesdell.

I forgot exactly how they did it, but it was, like, half of the time we would be in class and the other half we'd be in the principal's office, in the space they had designated for us. I think they did that during our recess time; they'd have us sit in the principal's office or inside a designated classroom to do schoolwork while the other students went outside to play. So, they still had us learning, no matter what. They made sure we got our work done even when we acted up.

For a minute, I was so crazy that I ended up running the streets around Truesdell. I was a wild boy on those streets. Or at least I thought I was. At the time, I thought that getting into trouble was what made you cool. So, if you met me between my fifth and seventh grade school years, you probably would've said, "That kid isn't going to make it. He's gonna end up dead."

I didn't even have my height yet. I was about five-six in the sixth grade. Then I got to about five-nine or five-ten later. But I was always long and lean. I was just a skinny brown kid, doing my thing with the T-Mob crew. We did that from the fifth grade to the seventh, and we carried it over to junior high school at Paul Public Charter. We got in a whole lot of trouble together too. As I stated earlier, some of us even got arrested, including me. *Twice.*

What happened on the first arrest was, we rode together about eight deep to this Northwest neighborhood off of 16th Street, where we could steal different things. On this particular day, we wanted to steal bikes that we would repaint and sell, or sell the bikes as is. However, somebody called the cops on us that day, before we could get away. The police ended up chasing us on our bikes. As usual, most of the guys got away; I just wasn't one of them that time. I got caught up, and my grandmother had to come and get me from the holding facility.

They had us in the same holding cells as they did the adults, but because we were juveniles, they put us in cells by ourselves, not with the adult prisoners. I still can't understand how everyone else got away and I didn't. It all just happened so *fast.* You know, with only three cops and a gang of us, they couldn't catch everybody. I guess the rest of my guys slipped through the cracks. So, me and BJ were the unlucky ones.

They took us down to the precinct, where I had to call my grandmother, and she couldn't even come and get me out until the next day. Like I said before, my grandmother was busy, with a lot going on, taking care of the whole family. She couldn't just jump up and come get me. But the next day, she was right there for me.

Man, I was mad, scared, and upset before she came to get me. But I didn't cry or anything. I was too busy trying to play the tough guy. BJ and I were just mad that we got caught.

"Damn, man, they got us!" is what kept coming out of our mouths.

I got out before BJ, though. My grandmother arrived to get me before his people came to get him. Like I said, my grandmother was *pissed* when she showed up to get me. She said, "You gotta be kidding me! You know better than that. You *know* better than that!" That's what she kept saying. "You *know* better than that, Vernon!" That's how mad she was. I definitely knew that I was about to get more from my grandfather when I got back home.

As soon as I walked into the house, Lynwood grabbed me by the shoulders and said, "Get your ass up in that room. You got your momma and me coming down to the police precinct to get you for doing some crazy stuff? What's wrong with you, boy? You know better than that shit!"

My grandfather didn't beat me. He just put his hands on me and told me to get my ass in my room, *quick*, and they took some of my privileges and stuff away from me that week. They told me that I couldn't go outside after school, and they took away my video games, along with some other things that were important to me.

But I didn't have a lot of material possessions in the first place. We were still poor. I mean, we weren't *dirt* poor, but we weren't well-off, that's for sure. My grandmother and grandfather worked to provide us with the best they could. Remember, they were providing for seven grandkids *and* some of their own children, our aunts and uncles. My grandmother was old-fashioned and didn't believe in breaking the mold with something that was out of character. She couldn't just jump up and buy me a bike. She had bills to take care of, as well as provide for all of her family members.

Back then, video games weren't that expensive. We're talking about an Atari, Intellivision, and Nintendo, which were all super-cheap in the 1980s and early 1990s. So, we had an Atari at the house, and I had a Nintendo game. My grandparents had enough to afford that for us. We would get these video games as gifts at Christmas, our birthday, or on some other special occasion. It was never just a random buy. It had to be for something special. Otherwise, they may have spoiled us.

My grandmother always got us nice things for Christmas, though. That was the main time of year when she would buy us things. That was when I would get a bike or a video game—whichever one I wanted. Then, I had other relatives who would send us gifts from time to time. They all knew how many of us there were, and that our mother was addicted to drugs. I guess some of our relatives felt sorry for us.

But yeah, when I got arrested that first time, my grandparents took my video games away from me and I couldn't go back outside for a while to hang out with my crew. As much fun as we *thought* we were having as T-Mob, we were really misguided kids who I would eventually have to grow away from. I would say the main thing we got off track with was stealing. When you grow up in the 'hood you'll do anything to get money. Well, not *anything*, but you'll do as much as you can. The teenagers and older guys were on the streets selling drugs, but as a young kid, you're going to try some other things to make money, like going to the corner stores to steal stuff to sell later.

I remember we used to head down to the Fourth District Precinct on Georgia Avenue and steal bikes; the police would confiscate motorbikes, which were illegal in DC, and hold them at their headquarters. They had a whole yard for them. We used to jump the wall at the precinct and take the bikes through an opening in the yard. I guess the police weren't thinking about anybody trying to steal from them right at the precinct. But we were bold enough to do it, and we never got caught.

We did some crazy stuff. But we didn't even try to sell the bikes we stole at the precinct. You might end up selling them to the same people they were taken away from. Really, we just wanted to ride them. When you can't afford them, and you want nice things, you're going to take them. I mean, everybody wants a nice dirt bike or motorbike and other cool stuff. Growing up in the 'hood, when you're on welfare, you can't afford any of that.

What we did was scope things out for days, as if we were on a police or military stakeout. We did this to figure out exactly how we were going to steal something. We used to ride by the precinct every day to see what everything looked like. We had the logistics mapped out. That's what you learn to do when you want stuff you can't afford. We weren't thinking about working for it yet. We were young kids, still wet behind the ears.

With all the bikes I used to steal, people started calling me "The Bike King." We even had a pair of bolt cutters to cut people's locks or snap their bike chains in half whenever they had them locked to a pole or a gate. We used to carry the bolt cutters in our backpacks and head to the local pool, where we'd cut locks and take bikes from kids who were swimming.

Looking back on it, we were vicious, man. We didn't care about anybody. We'd go and steal bikes at the pools, the parks, the playgrounds, outside the grocery stores, shopping centers, or wherever people would lock up a bike. That was back before people started using those U-locks that you can't break. Man, those U-locks are like *kryptonite.* We couldn't break those things no matter how hard we tried, but if someone used the little wire chains or a normal lock, their bike was easily stolen.

My bike stealing habit got so out of control that at one time, I had, like, twenty bikes in my grandmother's backyard, and she never even knew about it. We used to steal them and then spray-paint them so they wouldn't be recognized by their true owners. I used to stash bikes in the backyard under the porch. That's where I had a whole fleet of them. I had so many bikes that I used to change them up and ride a different one every day. I knew how to fix them inside and out because we stole so many different types.

That's where my being the oldest came in handy, because my younger brothers and sisters were never in my business. They knew better. I was much older than them and carried a lot of weight. When you live in a town house, you don't have the kind of backyard where you go out and just chill, with cookouts and other outdoorsy stuff. Our backyard was just a backyard, and nobody ever went back there. So, all of those bikes and other things that we stole would go right out in the back.

All of our criminal activities went down between fifth and seventh grades, during a crazy three-year span. In our tween years, I might have been the sharpest of the T-Mob as far as criminal activities were concerned. I guess I was the most ambitious and fearless. So, a lot of the stuff we did was my idea. One time, we rode all the way out to the suburbs of PG's County, in Maryland, to get into mischief, and that was pretty far for us.

If we planned to steal something, we'd usually ride six deep, where two guys could each ride on three bikes. We traveled on our missions that way, in case we found some bikes to steal. Then the extra riders would peddle the stolen bikes back. Somehow we always found bikes to steal. Bikes were everywhere. All we had to do was look for them. Our success rate was pretty good.

Then, as I said, I got arrested for a second time, out in Prince George's County, for trying to steal two puppies. They were two little Dobermans, I believe. One was brown and the other was black. We had gotten away with stealing dogs and selling them before, but not this time. We usually kept the stolen dogs at JuJu's house, like the puppy pit bulls we stole in DC.

Out in PG's County with the Dobermans, we were on our bikes, and we had the dogs in our hands. We got in and out of this suburban backyard with them fast too. You know, you jump over the fence, grab the dogs, and climb back over. The next thing we knew, after leaving the house with the dogs and getting around the corner, the Maryland police just pulled up on us from everywhere. They looked ready to run us over.

We jumped off the bikes and ran to get over a nearby hill. When we got over the hill, there was nowhere else for us to go. I guess the Maryland police knew that already. When we ran back over the hill to get away, the Maryland police had us cornered. And just like with my first arrest in DC, there were three officers after us, and some of the guys scattered in different directions and got away, while one of us didn't. Again, I was the one who didn't get away.

Like James Brown once said, "You gotta pay the cost to be the boss." I was now paying *twice*. Of course, by the time we came back to face the cops, we didn't have the dogs anymore. I think we dropped them and let them go as soon as we knew that we were cornered.

It was only about five of us out there that day. I found out later that a complaint was made in the area that someone had gone into a house and taken their dogs. I guess a neighbor must have spotted us and called the police. Even though we no longer had the dogs with us, the police already knew about it. Stealing dogs in Maryland was a felony.

It was crazy how it happened, though. We had five young guys out there in Maryland, with the police in hot pursuit of us from all angles, with some of us on bikes and others not. Once again, I ended up being the only one who got caught after jumping off a bike to try to get away. But then, I just stopped running.

I don't know why I stopped trying to get away. I think I might have been wondering if they'd shoot me. You know, they could have shot me in the back, as happens in so many Black movies we saw. That's why I think I stopped running. I just froze up.

They caught up with me and put the handcuffs on. Then they placed me inside a squad car to take me down to a Maryland precinct somewhere. When my grandmother came to get me out that second time, she threatened to send me back to live with my mother in Southeast. That was absolutely the last place I wanted to go when I was a kid. So, I said, "NO! I won't do it again. I *promise!*"

I was that terrified of living with my mother. I had it so *good* at my grandmother's house. When we got back home that day, my grandfather Lynwood just stared at me. He had something else in mind. When I walked into the house after my second arrest, my grandfather popped the belt on me a couple of times and hit me so hard and so fast that I made a football-like move to escape him. I ran right to my room and locked the door behind me. That's how I avoided getting a good beating that night. I mean, Lynwood tried to, but I wasn't going for it that day. I used to stay getting into trouble, so I didn't avoid all of my ass whoopings, just that one and a few others.

That next day, my aunt Pattie came over. And she didn't *play.*
That's even why they called her *Pattie.* She was known for bringing her belt and whipping us for being bad. But her real name
was Verona. Pattie walked into the house that next day, and I
didn't know that she was even there. So, I walked out of my
room to head downstairs, and she caught me slipping and
popped me with this big old belt she had.

I fell to the ground and looked up behind to beg her like a
baby. "Oh, Pattie, *stop*! Oh, Aunt Pattie, I won't do it again. I
won't do it again!"

Pattie used to roam the streets while strung out on drugs with
my mother before she got herself cleaned up. Then she became
a tough disciplinarian because she cared about us, and she
knew firsthand what was out there in the streets, and it was nothing nice.

She said, "Get your ass up!" and repeated it. "Get your ass up!"

When I got up, I ran right back to my room and shut the door
again.

That's the crazy type of predicament I was getting myself into
before I made my big transition at seventh grade. However, it
wasn't like a drastic change, where everything improved right
away. Mentally, I was making a slow transition. I was still hanging
out in the streets because we all liked to ride bikes. We used to
ride the BMX bikes and do all kinds of tricks with them,
like popping wheelies for a whole block without ever putting
the front wheel down.

We also liked to ride extra-fast and jump hills. Sometimes
people would stand on this one dirt hill, and I used to take the
bike hard and jump over them, Evel Knievel style. We did all
kinds of maneuvers on our bikes. And the more active I was on
bikes—doing a lot of tricks and general riding—the more
I stayed out of trouble in the streets. That's also when I started

focusing more on playing basketball and football. Eventually, I just stopped getting into trouble altogether and hung out with my boys on the block.

I graduated from Truesdell's sixth grade class in the summer of 1999, and JuJu and I remained best friends all the way up to seventh grade. Then we just fell off and started getting involved in different things, hanging out with different people. That's when I cut everything off with the whole T-Mob crew. But I wouldn't say I turned my back on anyone, I just stopped hanging out in the streets for my own good.

As it turned out, JuJu ended up dropping out of school in the seventh grade. He said he just didn't feel like he was into school anymore. That was the same year I started changing my own life and rededicating myself, with my focus on what I wanted to do. I definitely wasn't thinking about dropping out of school like JuJu did. I wanted to dedicate myself more to playing sports and doing what I was supposed to do in my classes without getting into trouble out in the streets. I wanted to stop those embarrassing and defiant years, where I made one bad decision after another, hurting my grandmother and the rest of the family. I was trying not to do that anymore.

Most of my friends didn't really trip about my change of interests, though. They all knew what I wanted to do already. I was ambitious about playing sports, and they could sense that I was trying to straighten out my life. Some of them even came out to see me when I played basketball in junior high, and then when I ran track and played ball in high school.

When I reached the sixth grade, I was already dunking on folks in basketball. In Washington, DC, we called it knocking. When I started dunking with full-court in junior high at Paul Public Charter, I became the *man* in basketball.

By eighth grade, I had grown to a new height of six-two and

was fast and strong. After that, the cheerleaders gave me a nick-name and made up a cheer for me. Imagine that! I had my own song. They were calling me Duke Duncan because I was banging on everybody with dunks down low. I could shoot a lit-tle bit, but I was more of a dunker and a bruiser inside the paint. Because of my size and strength, I played the power forward po-sition in junior high; you know, getting rebounds, blocking shots, and doing the dirty work under the basket. Actually, I was doing a little bit of everything, getting out on the fastbreaks, dunking, playing good defense. I was just *the man*, and one of the team's top scorers.

As I stated earlier, my family members didn't come out to a lot of my games. My grandmother was still hustling hard and taking care of my younger brothers and sisters, and even some of our cousins when she needed to. So, she didn't have a whole lot of free time. But I understood it. Like I said, she had a lot of people to take care of and to look after.

I just kept playing hard for the crowd and for myself, with new goals in mind to accomplish. As long as I was able to play ball, I was good. I didn't need anything extra. I was just doing what I liked to do and dominating. I would probably say that Alice Deal was one of our top competitor schools in the Northwest, over there by Woodrow Wilson High School and the Chevy Chase area.

Reflecting back, I had a lot of fun at Truesdell and Paul. Even though we got in trouble a lot, those were some of the best days of my life, just putting in dues with my friends. But you know, I would learn better than to get into so much trouble for the hell of it. That part of the fun was not good.

I remember my grandmother showing up at my graduation from Truesdell and then at my graduation from Paul, and her being extra-proud of me at both of them. We took a bunch of classmate pictures and all that good stuff, but there were totally different people that I hung out with at those two graduations.

At Paul Public Charter, I was older, wiser, more mature, and I was highly into sports. In fact, all of my teammates became my new friends. So, I had a totally different group of guys that I hung out and took pictures with when I graduated from Paul than when I graduated from Truesdell. Then I headed on to Dunbar Senior High School, where I had to make new friends again.

Chapter 4
Dunbar Senior High School

I MOVED ON FROM TRUESDELL ELEMENTARY AND PAUL CHARTER Junior High to attend Paul Laurence Dunbar Senior High School, at the bottom of Northwest, near Downtown in 2000, and graduated in 2003. I was in the tenth grade, and nobody really knew me there. I was more known at the top area of Northwest, what we called Uptown. I was supposed to go to Theodore Roosevelt High School, but I didn't want to be around the same people in my old neighborhood. I wanted to spread my wings in a new school and in a new environment.

Honestly, I didn't want to go to my neighborhood school. What I wanted to do was get away from all of my previous friends and everybody I had grown up with to get a fresh start. I had to get an out-of-boundary slip from the school district to go there.

I was just thinking outside the box. *If I go to Roosevelt, I'm going to be with all the guys I grew up with and I'll be tempted to get back into trouble. And if I go to Coolidge High School, I'll be around all the guys I grew up with there too.* You know, because Coolidge was not that far North from us. Staying close to home with my old friends didn't make sense to me anymore if I wanted to be on the straight and narrow. Sometimes being on the right side of the road means you need to change your direction for a whole new course of action. Because if my old classmates and neighborhood friends got into some mess in high school, and I was around them, I would've been in the same mess with them because we grew up together. It would have been guilt by association, and probably I would have gotten into something to protect my friends. I couldn't just stand there and watch. So, I figured the best thing to do was to leave the whole area to stay away from any of those situations.

However, when it was all said and done, nobody really cared about my decision not to stay in the neighborhood. Going to whatever high school was no big deal to my friends. My mother never really paid attention to what I did in school. My grandmother just wanted me to do what I wanted to do. So, I packed up and went to Dunbar, where the coaches didn't know me yet. The players didn't know me, nor did any of the students at the school. Nobody knew me. It was a brand-new challenge, almost like moving to a new city, and I was ready for it.

Whether the coaches or players knew me or not, I was going to Dunbar to make an impact. As soon as I got there, football season started. I remember we began practicing in the summertime. But honestly, I was going to Dunbar to focus on basketball. Remember, I hadn't played that much organized football yet, so I had more faith in basketball.

When I walked into the basketball gym at Dunbar, I saw that they had their starting five players already. They already knew one another, and it was obvious the coach had a little favoritism thing going on. When I saw that, I thought to myself, *You know what? I'm gonna try out for football.* And that's what I did.

I walked right up to the office of the head coach for football and knocked on the door. The door was already open, so I walked right in.

I said, "How are you doing, Coach? Can I try out for the football team?"

He looked at me and said, "Yeah, sure, sure. What's your name, son?"

"My name is Vernon. Vernon Davis."

Then he asked me, "What position are you trying to play?"

"Anything that has to do with scoring touchdowns," I answered with confidence.

The coach nodded and remained serious. He took me seriously from day one.

He said, "All right, all right. We'll see what you can do."

He was a Black coach named Craig Jefferies, and was still pretty young at the time. I think he was around fortyish when I first got there. That was still pretty young for a head coach. You know, most coaches like to keep their jobs for a while and grow old with them. But Coach Jefferies was young, and he was *big* too. I think he played ball at Cheyney University.

Well, I walked into his office in the heat of the summer, when all of the athletes were already in training. Basketball even had a summer league. That's how sports were. You would start training early to get a jump on coming together and playing well as a team and individually during the season. The work started way before the season. Guys were basically working out, training, or doing something else to improve their athletic skills all year long.

I remember my first time out there on the field with the varsity boys at Dunbar. Coach Jefferies put me out there to run, jump up the bleachers, and do other practice drills. They were just, like, the start of team drills, you know. They wanted to see what kind of physical shape you were in and how much work you could take.

So, I got out there on the track that surrounds the field, all six-three and 205 pounds of me. I'm out there as this big, young boy, and I'm running past everybody, like they're stuck in quicksand. I'm, like, superathletic already. Even the strength and conditioning coach was impressed by me.

He said, "Damn! This boy is killing it!"

Everyone was impressed with me. They just kept saying, "Damn, where the hell did this kid come from?" Nobody could figure me out because I didn't go to school with any of their guys and I didn't live in their neighborhoods. In their minds, I was just this kid who had walked off the street with crazy potential. Other than that, they didn't know a thing about me. All they knew was that I was young and superathletic. I was pretty determined too. I wasn't going to Dunbar to sit on the team bench. I wanted to *play* right away, and I knew I was good enough, so I had to show it.

We did wind sprints and all kinds of other physical drills. We were running around cones and obstacles, jumping, bending, crawling, getting back up, and sprinting again. It was like we were in the military, US Marines. And I was crushing all of it, dominating everything with raw athleticism in the tenth grade. I've just always been pretty fast. I even ran track and did the high jump at Dunbar.

Well, after the first couple of football practices, the coaches were going crazy. I don't remember everything they said, but I know they were excited about me. "We're going to put you at tight end," they told me. I hadn't really thought about the position I would play before that. I just wanted to get the ball in my hands, however I could, to score some touchdowns. But they put me right in at tight end.

Then Coach Jefferies started speaking to me differently. He was giving me more respect and recognition. He asked me, "You feel like you can play this position?" He was talking about being the team's starting tight end again. So, I was, like, "Yeah," and there was no backup tight end behind me. So, I was it. That first year, we had a really good team.

The next thing you know, I was the new kid on the block

again and ready to blow up at the tight end position. Then they had me on the receiving and kickoff teams because they knew that I was fast and always ready to fly up the field. They even created special plays for me, to make sure I got the ball in my hands.

Man, in that tenth grade year, I was unstoppable. They had me playing more than just tight end. They even put me at defensive end, right across from the other team's tight end. I was all over the field, playing everything. After that, all of the colleges wanted me. I was still only a sophomore.

I was very dominant on the field, though, and dominance didn't have an age. Either you can compete on the level you need to or you can't. I actually don't remember a lot of the details of my first games. It was all a fast-moving blur. I only scored maybe seven or eight touchdowns that year, but I was still a big playmaker. I would get big chunks of yards every time I touched the ball. In high school, unless you're the starting and featured running back, you may only touch the ball seven or eight times a game, if *that*. So, you had to make every play count.

We made it to the championship game that year too. And we won it. I think we played against Howard Dilworth (H.D.) Woodson that first year. In Washington, DC, we called the championship game the Turkey Bowl, played around Thanksgiving time. In fact, I think we won it every year that I was at Dunbar.

I had a new girlfriend at Dunbar too. I had broken up with all of my previous girlfriends in middle school and junior high. Man, let me tell you, Dunbar had some hot girls! Some of the hottest girls in DC went to Dunbar when I was there, and they still do now. Dunbar is where I first started dating a girl named Janel. But she wasn't the same Janel who I ended up living with and later on having children with. She was the first Janel I dated from Dunbar.

I had pretty good grades in my first year, which qualified me to play any and all sports. I think my favorite subject was Spanish, with Ms. Wolfolk. After that first year on the team, the students and faculty at Dunbar either knew me or knew *of* me. I think the biggest advantage I had in tenth grade was being unknown and just blowing the team away with my raw skills. When people don't know you, they can't game plan for you. You know, you weren't on their radar. So, that earned me a lot of respect from my teammates.

To top things off in a great first year, we had Josh Cribbs leading us as our quarterback. He ended up making the pros, not as a quarterback but as a return specialist for the Cleveland Browns. The man was a *beast* in high school. Just imagine Josh Cribbs with the ball in his hands on every play, where he could keep it, hand it off to someone else, or pass it. If you don't know who Josh Cribbs is, look up some of his Cleveland Browns highlights on YouTube.

We also had a guy named Darrell Dowry on the team who played wide receiver. He was fast, with good hands and about six feet tall. When you can catch and run great routes, you become the ideal receiver for football. That's what Darrell was for us. In fact, he and Josh were both recruited to play college ball at Kent State. You know, when the college scouts were coming out to see Josh, they fell in love with Darrell and a few of the older guys on the team too. And they all got to see me. Because of that early attention to my game, I started getting early scholarship offers, even though I had two years left before graduation.

I had Josh Cribbs to thank for all of that extra attention. Without Josh being heavily recruited from the colleges, and without our team doing so well, no one would have been there to see me go off. Because of Josh and the winning program that Coach Jefferies was building at Dunbar, the college scouts all got a chance to see me early. I was still making my own noise, so the scouts would have eventually come out to see me anyway. Josh Cribbs just sped up the pace for me. And I thank him for it.

After football season was over, I went right back to playing basketball, and right after basketball, I ran track. So, I went back-to-back-to-back in sports, and just stayed busy working my athletic body. When I transitioned from football and got myself ready for the basketball team, the guys there were just as amazed as the football ones at how I could move the way I did as a big man. I was just as fast on the basketball court, hustling up and down the court, as I was on the football field.

At six-three, 220 pounds, I was a big, strong guy to deal with. Of course, some of the guys on the basketball team were taller than me, but they weren't as solid or as strong as I was. You know, football is more about weight and power than basketball. I had weight and power from football, which translated into me being able to move and handle guys on the basketball floor.

I came off the bench in basketball as the sixth or seventh man as a power forward and went right to grabbing rebounds, playing good defense, and of course, running the floor. I don't think I started in basketball until my senior year, but I still played a lot. In fact, I got a lot of playing time even without starting.

We were also good in basketball at Dunbar. In fact, all three years that I was there, we were good, just like in football. We had a kid named Tre Kelley in basketball who came in when I did, and he improved his skills every year, just like I did in football. So, we were competing for city league championships in basketball as well, my first, second, and third year at Dunbar. Tre Kelley was killing it, which ended up landing him at South Carolina. When the springtime came around for track-and-field, I ran the 100 meters, of course. Then I ran the 4 x 100 relay, and I did the high jump. I did well in every event, too. It was funny sometimes because I would line up to race and the other track guys would look at me like I was crazy. They'd be thinking, *Who is this big boy lining up to run with us?* And they'd be blown away whenever I smoked them. So, I loved it, the whole idea of taking people off guard and surprising them.

I participated in a lot of different track-and-field events. They even had me throw the shot put a few times. I killed that event too. On the relays, I would either start the race strong or take the anchor leg and finish it. Some people thought I would wear myself out with all of those events, especially after playing basketball and football in the same school year. But I didn't get worn out. I was just an active and athletic kid. I just wanted to play ball and stay busy.

Like I said, I *loved it*! I loved everything about competing. I even liked the little nervousness and butterflies you got when you lined up for track. It just let you know that you had a race to run. The icing on the cake for me was that all of the sports kept me out of trouble.

Honestly, I don't think it was anything in particular about track-and-field that I liked. I just knew that in order to be great at what I wanted to do, I had to do more than just play football. In my opinion, every great athlete had speed, and they competed in more sports than just one.

Look at Bo Jackson and Deion Sanders. Both of those guys are still known as superathletes today because they excelled in both professional football and baseball. Take Josh Cribbs for instance; he played quarterback and he was a hell of an athlete, man. It seemed like he competed in every single sport we had at the school, including swimming, track, basketball, and football.

I mean, when it came to sports, Dunbar had the school spirit behind us all—the cheerleaders, parents, DC news reporters, and the college scouts were all coming out to the games in waves and cheering us on. Everyone was coming out to see and support us for the entire year. The crowds kept getting thicker and thicker, including Otis, who showed up in the stands to watch me. He was, like, the only one I could count on from the family to come out. Sometimes he brought family and other people with him, including my brother Vontae.

After tenth grade, I broke up with my first high school girlfriend and met another girl named Janel Horn, who I ended up living with in the eleventh and twelfth grades. Janel eventually became the mother of my three children.

Once my little brother saw me excelling in high school sports, he really started paying attention to me and began to work out with me a bit more. When my eleventh grade season hit, my game elevated again, raised to another level. There was no more of me being unknown at that point. The whole city knew who I was: the coaches, the media, the college scouts—everyone was showing up at our high school.

During that second year at Dunbar, we had some other top-flight guys who came in to play with us, like Michael Davis. He played everything: quarterback, receiver, safety. We had a new running back, Charles Cobb, and a full back in that second year as well. We just had more *talent* all across the board. We had a crazy tough defense too. They even moved me back to free safety in my second year on defense to help out against the big plays. Because I was a big guy who could run fast, and a ball hawk who could catch, the coaches figured no one could get past me back there. If they put the ball in the air, I'm going to get it. I could also run downhill from the safety spot and nail you with my size on a running play.

We went to our second straight Turkey Bowl championship game that year. During my first year, we beat Frank W. Ballou High School 35–12, then we played H.D. Woodson that second year and barely won. I think the score was like 16–14, and we had to come back from behind. They played us a good game, man. It would have been a big disappointment and an upset if we had lost because we were considered the better team.

Once I started getting my first official looks and letters from colleges, some of the first coaches who wanted me were local, the University of Maryland and the University of Virginia. Those coaches came after me immediately, in tenth grade. When I hit the eleventh, other colleges started to come, where I had, probably like twenty-five to thirty offers, including Florida, which I wasn't expecting.

Everybody who had a major program wanted me. So, I had interest from all the big schools, like Alabama, Georgia, Ohio State, and Michigan. I can't even remember all of them. I only went on four college visits, with the University of Florida being on that list, because I liked the weather down there. Then I took a visit to Purdue, Virginia, and Maryland, to be close to home. But I never selected a fifth school to visit. I was only interested in those four.

I became so recognized and celebrated for my skills in DC that I was named a US Army All-American, which means they take some of the top high players in the country and pull them all together to play in a national football game. I ended up playing in one of those games my senior year, and I was one of the top players in the country.

After playing football in the eleventh grade, I went back to playing basketball with another inch, which made me six-four. That was my final height for college and the pros. I guess I weighed under 230 pounds at that time. But that's rock-solid size for high school.

I ran track again in my junior year at Dunbar, with sprints, the high jump, and the 4 x 100 relay. By my senior year, I was one of the fastest sprinters in the city, with a 10.7 in the 100 meters. I did really well in the high jump too. With my height, size, and speed, I jumped 6 feet 6 inches and set an all-time DCIAA record that still remains in the books in DC.

My girlfriend, Janel Horn, was with me through all of it. She was tall, very athletic, limber, and light-skinned, like my mother. Yeah, she was another yellow girl. We ended up being with each other for a long time, actually. We finally split up in 2016, after having three kids and spending sixteen years together.

I don't know what it was, but it seemed like I always dated light-skinned girls. Maybe that had something to do with the idea of being comfortable with and attracted to girls who re-minded me of my mother—without the drug addictions, of course. I think this girl named Angel Anderson, who ended up going to Woodrow Wilson High School, was the only girl I was with who wasn't yellow. I think that was during my last year at Paul, in junior high school. I remember she had two brothers I was cool with.

Speaking of my mom, I didn't see her as much once I headed off to high school. She never came to the games like Otis did. Neither my grandmother nor anyone else could force me to go see her at her place in Southeast anymore. I was no longer around the Petworth area, so I didn't have to see her walking around fiending, like a zombie. So, I no longer had to worry about being embarrassed.

Otis continued to come to my football and basketball games throughout my whole high school career. My games were, like, the highlight of his week. He even made it out to some of my track meets in the spring. I really appreciated him for that. It would always be too many people out there at the games and the track meets for my mother to feel comfortable. Nor did she like people trying to hit or tackle me in football. She was similar to my grandmother in that regard. They just didn't want anyone to hurt their boy.

The way our high school schedules were set up, we had games in the daytime, right after school let out. So, you would basically have to be off work in the early afternoon to catch a game, un-less you worked nights. That left most of the games for the home crowd only, and that stopped the neighborhood fights and other street drama that could go on at nighttime. We did have opposing crowds for the playoffs and, of course, for the Turkey Bowl championship game, which had DC police every-where.

At the time, my girlfriend Janel was all-in with me; that's how

I got to live with her and her family. She would be with me at the games, the after-parties, at school, at home, and everywhere I went. A lot of girls couldn't deal with all of the stuff I had going on. I even kept a little job to keep money in my pocket, while playing all these different sports.

I was so in love with Janel, and she was so in love with me, that we were around each other all the time. So, her parents and family got to love me too. I mean, I was over at her house every single day, and I used to sneak over there at night. I remember Janel used to act like she was closing the door at night, but then I wouldn't leave. I would chill behind the bed and stay there with her.

So, after a while, it was like, "You just want to stay over here? You're here every day anyway."

I was, like, "Yeah." Then I just moved out of my grandmother's house with my clothes and went to live with Janel and the Horn family. That's how it happened. But, you know, I was still around my grandmother and family when I needed to be.

Janel Horn ended up being the love of my life for a long time because she was really into me. You know, some girls want you to be more about them, and I really didn't have the time to do that. So, a lot of girls that I dated would break up with me. I never remember breaking up first with any of them. They would always want to leave me because they didn't feel I had enough time for them.

By eleventh grade, I also had some wheels to get around in. My grandmother bought me a gold Tahoe Jeep to drive to school, to work, and wherever else I needed to go. So, I was set. My life looked *great*, and I was working my tail off to keep adding more to it. I was hungry to succeed and not become another drug-addicted failure in DC. Because they were all over the place, especially where I grew up.

Then I had my senior year, when I decided to just go to Maryland so that my family and friends could still come out to see my games or just watch them on TV. The local college games would always come on our local networks. That way, my people would be able to see me every week if I went to Maryland or Virginia. So, I just decided to commit to Maryland. Really, I knew I was going to Maryland by the end of the eleventh grade. But I didn't say anything to confirm it until after my senior year of football. That's when everyone else would announce their college choices.

By my senior year, I was superdominant. We went all the way to the championship game again, but this time we finally lost 19–3 to H.D. Woodson, the same school we beat the year before. Even though we lost the championship game in my final year at Dunbar, the team was still stacked for the next run.

We had a young wide receiver named James McDonald, who was an absolute *freak*. He was two years younger than me and about six-two, with speed, great hands, and long arms. He became a star for us as soon as he took the field. They went back to the championship and won two more Turkey Bowls, over Ballou and H.D. Woodson again. I think McDonald ended up going to Penn State.

Then we had a quarterback named Stanford Brown who could run a little bit, but he was more of a passer. On defense, we had a guy named Luke Kane who played strong safety, while I continued to play free safety. We just couldn't bring it all together that day to win another championship my senior year.

After everything was said and done at Dunbar, my first year was probably my favorite, when nobody knew me and I got to break out on the scene for everybody in DC. With Josh Cribbs as quarterback, we were blowing teams out that year, and even blew out Ballou in the Turkey Bowl. We were just stronger as a team that first year, so everything came easier for us.

In my senior year of basketball, I finally got to start at power forward. I was already committed to playing football long term, so playing basketball was just out of fun for me that final year; I already knew I had a future in football.

We had a guy on the basketball team that year who had gotten way better in his skills by our senior year. He was Tre Kelley, and he came to Dunbar the same year that I did. He was a six-foot point guard who could handle the ball in traffic, as well as shoot.

Tre was like, the *best*. He was really a good player who could score in a lot of different ways. And the girls all loved him. He was *the man*! I think he took the scoring title in DC for both our junior and senior years. Then we beat Cardoza, 75–62 for the DC public school title that last year. So, we were champions in basketball too.

Tre committed to the University of South Carolina and became a big basketball story, with reports about his mother being beaten and killed by an angry lover when he was young. He never talked about that, so you would never know it happened. It was one of his motivating factors to play ball so hard, to please his mother in heaven.

That's just how tough life was for a lot of us coming up in DC. I was going hard myself, motivated by my own mother and her issues. You know, I still loved her, I just needed to understand her more. In the meantime, I didn't want my life to end with a sad story, so I kept on pushing just like Tre Kelley did.

Those were my high school days, filled with excelling in sports at Dunbar: football, basketball, and track-and-field. I had a name, an athletic crew of friends, and a dedicated girlfriend whom I lived with. I had no fights and no worries. Overall, life had been pretty good for me in high school. *Very* good.

I remember walking through the school hallways with my head held up high with pride. I had two black-and-red Dunbar letterman jackets that I wore with our school colors. One had white sleeves with a black and red body, and I had another one with red sleeves. They had our names on our chest, with the big school decal, and our numbers, positions, nicknames, or whatever else you wanted to put on it. I used to switch them up and let Janel wear one to school or to the games when she wanted to.

Man, high school was *big fun*! All of the teachers and students knew who I was and gave me love. I didn't hang out that much in the streets, though; I was just too busy. We got invited to all the parties. I stayed out of trouble while on my way to Maryland in the hopes of a professional football career.

I remember some of my teammates used to call me Burnie, like Vernon the Burner, because I was so fast. My main hang-out buddies were probably Larry Brown, who played on the offensive line. And my boy Chris Gates, who played on the offensive line. He was superpopular and was a good player too. And I had my boy, Marcel Ward, who played wide receiver on the team. We all hung out together in school. Marcel's mom used to pick me up to drive me to school every morning before I got my first car and moved in with Janel, her parents, and her older brother.

Again, thanks to my grandmother allowing the school system to hold me back a year at Truesdell, it paid off with more maturity when I got into high school. I also took precollege courses to prepare for that next level of education at Maryland. To her credit, my grandmother just knew how important it was for me not to shortcut the educational process. So, I thank her again, and again, and again for her tough love, because when it was all said and done, my high school experience was a great one!

Off the field, Coach Craig Jefferies became like a father figure to me. He used to talk to me all the time about my workouts, and he even drove me to a few when I worked out for the University of Virginia. Coach would sign me up and take me to a lot of the football camps that were anywhere near us. It was, like, whenever anyone had a football camp, Coach Craig would call me up to take me. So, I had a lot of DC angels on my side to make sure that I won in the bigger game of life and was able to move on and do what I aspired to do.

Some of the craziest memories I had from Dunbar Senior High were when the Pentagon got hit in September 2001. We were all sitting in class when we saw the smoke in the distance; then everybody started staring out the window. Everyone in school was going crazy, thinking that terrorists were ready to attack us and everyone else in DC. They dismissed us from school early that day, giving everyone a chance to head home for safety. It was just *crazy*!

I also remember the DC sniper attacks in October 2002. Everyone was scared to stop for gas around the city. That was a crazy experience too. I had my car by then and was looking over my shoulders at the gas stations. It was as if this guy could shoot you from anywhere.

Despite how it may seem, with me naming a lot of guys who went off to college that I knew and played ball with, not a lot of us athletes in DC got the opportunity to attend the big-time Division I schools in football. We had more kids getting D-I letters for basketball. Not even Josh Cribbs got a big school football scholarship. He ended up going to Kent State and made it to the NFL from there a year before me, in 2005, when the Cleveland Browns picked him up as a nondrafted kick and punt returner.

So, it was a big deal when my guy Luke Kane went off to the University of Syracuse. Syracuse was a major university at that time because of basketball. But like I said, even though I was recruited by all the big-time football schools myself, I decided to stay close to home and go to Maryland so my family could watch me play.

I mean, I probably could have been closer to winning a championship at Florida, who played in the SEC (Southeastern Conference) with Alabama, LSU, Auburn, and Georgia, but I was satisfied with being at Maryland. I just didn't see the same opportunity for my family to come to watch me play if I went farther away, to Florida or Purdue.

At the end of the day, Maryland, in the ACC (Atlantic Coast Conference) with Florida State, Clemson, Virginia Tech, Notre Dame, and Miami, still got me to the NFL as a top 10 draft pick. So, Maryland wasn't a bad choice for me at all. I think it was a *good* choice. I now have friends for life who went to school with me and were my teammates at the University of Maryland.

Chapter 5
University of Maryland

AS I SAID, I CHOSE TO ATTEND THE UNIVERSITY OF MARYLAND TO further my education and play ball where my friends and family could see me every weekend if they wanted to. However, I was very tempted by Florida for the nice weather down there. I also looked at Purdue and the University of Virginia.

Aside from the nice weather, I thought Florida had a great team. Not only that but Coach Mike Locksley, who recruited me to Maryland, ended up heading down to Florida to become one of Coach Ron Zook's assistants.

I was attracted to Purdue because of how badly they were trying to recruit me. They were showing me a lot of love and interest, and they needed a tight end they could play in a multitude of ways. That really made me fall in love with the school, and the whole idea of being a part of a tight-end heavy program. They really valued the tight end position.

On the other hand, Virginia I respected because of all the initial love they showed me while I was still in the tenth grade. They were highly interested in me. They were planning on utilizing me in a big way, and I thought it would be a great fit. Plus, I would be close to home. But Maryland was even closer, and I wanted to be near my grandmother.

I was also loyal to Maryland because I grew up watching them on local TV every time I saw that one of their games was on. From watching the Terrapins on TV, I loved the coliseum they played in, and the Maryland state colors they wore on their helmets and jerseys. Coach Ralph Friedgen seemed like a really loyal guy who I could play for and trust. I went in as a freshman in the early summer of 2003. I think it may have been in June, right after graduating from high school, because they had a summer workout and early training program, so I had to hurry up and get there. I had already been on the campus, and it wasn't that far from home, so I was very comfortable there.

There was a summer orientation program for all incoming freshmen, including the new recruits. We all had to arrive at school early to get situated and acclimated. I had a roommate, but I can't remember who it was that first year. We were in a dorm room on campus. I do remember our room being super-small, though. You know, with football players being some of the biggest guys on campus, it's kind of hard to put us in small dorm rooms, but that's what happens your freshman year. You come in like a regular student, but you have to do all of your football stuff and extra training to get ready for the season.

I remember we all had to walk down the hallways to get to the showers and the bathrooms. Inside the rooms, the beds were so close together, you could barely walk in there. Then we had a nightstand in between the beds. I had roommates before in high school, whenever I spent a weekend at a football camp, so it wasn't that new of an experience for me. In college, we had to spend a whole semester in that small room. That was totally different. I wasn't really expecting that, but you got used to it, unless you were able to afford living off campus your freshman year. The coaches and counselors didn't really want you living off campus as a freshman; they wanted you to get close to your teammates and be around campus just in case you needed help with anything.

We all met up with our coaches: the head coach, the coordinators, the position coaches, and the trainers who would be working with us to get our bodies in peak condition. All of the coaches embraced us. I think we had an incoming class of twenty or so freshmen from all over the country. They also had an academic study hall set up for us to keep our grades in order.

We went right to doing drills that early summer because college games start in late August and we had to get ready. Outside of my roommate, I remember the first guy I met was Patrick Powell from Richmond, Virginia, a defensive end. I remember him having every jersey known to man. He had NFL football jerseys, NBA basketball, and college football jerseys all up in his closet. He pretty much had a whole jersey store in there. He was obviously a collector who took his collection seriously. So, I walked into his room, saw all of his jerseys hanging up in the closet, and we became good friends.

Patrick eventually moved in with me a little while after I got drafted and we started working together on business ideas. He then became my business manager, pretty much the way Lebron James linked up with Rich Paul, who formed Klutch Sports. I embraced a lot of the guys at Maryland as my teammates and brothers, and they embraced me. We spent a great deal of time together in college. Since you're on campus and inside the dorms, it's not like you get to go home after practice. At the end of the day, you're still on campus with those guys. You eat, sleep, drink, shower, work out, and do homework with them. So, we all got acquainted with one another on and off campus.

Patrick had all those jerseys, including a few Maryland jerseys, and I wanted to wear one to go back to the Turkey Bowl in DC that year. Dunbar was in the city championship football game again. So, I asked Patrick point-blank, "Dude, can I get this one? Can I borrow this jersey?"

I wanted to show off my University of Maryland colors at the game. Patrick was cool and let me borrow it. Then he ended up letting me keep it. For me, that was a big deal because I never really owned a jersey. My grandmother wasn't buying jerseys for me in grade or in high school, and I never bought one for myself. So, for me, that was really a significant moment in my life. Patrick and I have been diehard friends ever since.

Of course, at the college level, even though we went to several straight city championship games in DC with Dunbar, the college practices and games were much harder and different from high school, and the coaches expected more out of us. At the high school level, it's not like you're recruiting guys from all over the city to play for you. You basically work with whoever you have at the school who comes out for the team. However, at the college level, you recruited these guys from different places to play for you, and you have much higher expectations for the players. The coaches want you to run harder, jump higher, and throw farther.

Different parts of life have higher and different levels of demands and expectations. Everything in life has different levels. Whether you go from grade school or junior high school to high school, there are always different levels involved. So, you have to kick it up a notch.

I went from 5,000 people watching me play in DC to more than 50,000 at Maryland. That's when people expect more out of you, based on your past abilities and what you've become as a playmaker. You know what I mean? Athletically, mentally, strength wise, just more of everything is expected. College was on a whole different level.

The practices and the work weren't really that strenuous to

me, because we all played ball and were used to working out. You could just *feel* the difference in that next level up. You could tell that you were in a different space in college. It was a different phase of your career, like anything else in life that you go through.

Coach Friedgen was very tough too. He didn't take the nonsense. He was a "Yes, sir!" kind of coach who wanted you to take him seriously. He didn't want you taking him lightly, and he wouldn't take things lightly with you. So, if he sees you walking, he's going to get on you for it. If he sees you taking off on a play, he's going to yell at you and make you run gassers. Our head coach was always on you.

Then I had a position coach for tight ends, Coach Ray Rychleski, and it seemed like he was just hard on *me*. He was always pushing to get more out of me. I couldn't take off any play around him. He wanted me to go hard on every play, with no excuses. So, I didn't have any excuses. I had to step up to the plate and play my best ball.

Coach Ray wanted to develop me into a great player. He was *always* hard on me. When I missed a block in my first year, he told me, "You should have gone to Florida with Coach Mike Locksley." He actually told me that. He was a bald-headed white guy with a lot of swagger. Coach Ray is still there at Maryland now, after all these years.

Of course, college ball was going to be tough initially, but once you adapt to the new level of expectations and difficulties with optimism and patience, you know you can get through it because you've done it all before. Through more repetitions and hard work, you can become really good at it.

In that first year at Maryland, we had a guy on the team named Shawne Merriman, who was born in DC, but he had moved out to Upper Marlboro, where he became a legend out there on defense. He played outside linebacker and defensive end, where he would really get after the quarterback for us. Shawne was a big, strong, and fast man. He was a total freak on defense. They even called him "Lights Out" in high school when he knocked four different guys unconscious in the same game.

I wouldn't say that Shawne was faster than me, but he was just as tall and packed more weight at the time. He could also jump out of the gym and played basketball in high school like I did. So, he was just as athletic. Shawne ended up being drafted by the San Diego Chargers in 2005. He left school to go pro after his junior year just like I did, and he went on to win the NFL's defensive ROY (Rookie of the Year) that year. He was just an athletic marvel at the linebacker position, and he played that way for us at Maryland.

Another standout at Maryland was Josh Wilson, who played cornerback, starting from his freshman year. He was pretty good too and ended up being drafted by the Seattle Seahawks a year after me in 2007.

I remember one of the toughest games we had during my freshman year was against the Temple Owls up in Philadelphia. They had some big boys who could really hit. Temple even tried to recruit me before I made my choice of Maryland. We already had a pretty good tight end when I got there at Maryland, so I couldn't start my first year. We had a guy named Rob Abiamiri, who was pretty good. He had very good hands and was a great route runner. I don't think he made the pros. I believe he got a shot with a tryout, but I don't think he made it onto a roster. He may have made it to a training camp, but he didn't make it onto a team.

I don't recall all of the details of my freshman year, but what does stand out is that we made it to the Gator Bowl and won it in Florida. I think we played West Virginia and beat them pretty badly. I think the score was, like, fortysomething to seven. We got off to a fast start and never let up. I even had a great highlight reel play when they threw me a pass and I made, like, six guys miss. They put me in the game late and threw me a twelve-yard pass, and I just took off with it for another twenty yards. It was a great play—maybe the greatest one of my life—at that time, of course. That was the first and only time I really had a chance to get my hands on the ball that freshman year. And it ended up being in a bowl game.

I was mostly used on the kickoff and returns teams that freshman year, so what I did was perfect getting down the field and making some tacos by steamrolling guys. I probably had so many tacos on kickoff because I couldn't play anything else. A taco is when you outright flatten a guy, and I did that plenty of times. I had to be good at something, and because I played safety in high school, I still knew how to tackle. I would take off running on the kickoff team and just smash guys.

I had a nice level of notoriety from my high school days at Dunbar, but nothing really happened for me individually at Maryland in that freshman year. Everything catapulted for me in my second year as a sophomore. That's when I played more. I made more plays, and I started gaining traction again. Everybody started to become familiar with me on the college level.

For that second year, they had me doing a lot of different things to get the ball to me. I would roll out of the backfield and into the flats because they knew I could run once I got my hands on the ball. But it's not like I got a lot of plays at the tight end position. I would only touch the ball about four or five times a game. They didn't throw it to me that much. They had other guys to feed, like our running back, Lance Ball, and the wide receiver, Derrick Fenner. I felt pretty good about my second year, though. I felt like I got a lot tougher, especially after going up against guys like Shawne Merriman at practice every day. I could feel myself getting better when going up against Shawne. I had to be prepared for him because he was that good.

Shawne and I used to go at it at practice all the time. He was really tough to deal with. Guys would even form a circle around us when we went against each other; they knew they were about to get a show. I had to get better because I got tired of him kicking my butt. I mean, he really used to wear me out at practice. I still talk to Shawne and keep in touch with him. He had a hell of a career.

My breakout games in that sophomore year came against Duke, Virginia, and Florida, where I racked up a hundred yards in each game and scored three touchdowns in the Duke game. We had a bad season overall and never made it back to a bowl game. Nevertheless, even when we lost games, the energy in the stadium was electric. The fans and students were really into it, with the marching bands and everything.

Once I started to play more in my sophomore year, I fell right in rhythm with our quarterback, Joel Statham. He didn't make it to the pros or anything, but he sure put the ball on the money to me. But again, we didn't do that well as a team that year. You have to win at least six or seven games to qualify for a bowl day, and we didn't do that.

However, I gained more respect in my sophomore year and started to live up to a lot of the hype and expectations that people had for me. I only had a few touchdowns that year, but I still made an impact. I didn't have any crazy numbers as far as big plays go, but I definitely made my presence felt for the future. You could tell the coaching staff was planning to utilize me more in the years to come.

If my sophomore year was considered an elevation, things *really* took off for me in my junior year. That's when they expanded my role and had me playing everywhere to get me the ball even more. I would go from the left side to the right side, split out wide, stay in tight, fill in the slot, and even slide into the backfield sometimes. We had a new quarterback that year too,

Sam Hollenbeck. We still didn't have a great record, though, and we didn't make it to another bowl game.

For some reason, I seemed to play my best ball against the best competition in the ACC that year. I had standout games against Clemson, West Virginia, North Carolina, and North Carolina State that year, with five or more receptions, over 100 yards, and a touchdown in each game. I think I finished the year with six or seven touchdowns, fiftysomething receptions, and almost 900 yards.

After that junior year, there was a lot of buzz floating around about me being a first-round draft pick. I had made a lot of big highlight plays that year, so people started talking about me elevating to the next level again. This time it was the professional level. Even though I didn't break 1,000 yards receiving, the scouts could still see my ability enough to project me as a first-round draft pick.

During all three years at Maryland, I still had the same girlfriend. I didn't live with Janel and her family anymore, but she would come and see me on campus. Then I moved out of the dorms and had my own apartment on campus with a couple of new roommates, Derek Turner and Garrett McPherson, who were both on the football team with me. That's when Janel would come and stay with me sometimes. You had some football guys who got busted for dating different girls, but I was pretty focused on just playing football when I was at Maryland, and it paid off.

I don't really remember a lot of guys getting into trouble with drinking, fights, and all that kind of stuff. I mean, we couldn't control guys who got into slipups here and there, whether it was someone missing practice or getting into fights. Our team was mostly about playing football.

I remember it took a minute for me to get acclimated to the whole college environment at Maryland. It was a different world for me—no pun intended. While growing up in DC I never went to school with kids of different ethnicities. We had a few Hispanics, but not enough to pay that much attention to them. So, with me going from inner-city schools that were predominantly Black to a major college with different races, classes, and cultures, where Black students only made up 5 percent of the population, with the majority of the students being White, that was a bit of a culture shock.

I even had to improve my speech in college, because I spoke like I was straight out of DC. Many people couldn't understand my speech pattern and DC slang at first, because the dialect was a bit different. It's still English, but different cities have different ways of talking, especially among Black people. If you call yourself hard-core, then you're most likely going to have a strong inner-city dialect. Then you had football players coming from all over the place—Atlanta, Pennsylvania, Mississippi, Arkansas, Connecticut. They had different dialects as well, with their accents and their slang, just like I did.

I became good friends with all of the freshmen football players at Maryland, all the guys I came in with. We were all friends and became a close-knit group. Of course, me and Patrick had that extra connection because of him gifting me with my first-ever jersey. Patrick played defensive end, right on the other side from me. So, we went up against each other plenty of times at practice. We would bring out the best in each other.

Then there was Brandon Nixon, who played on the offensive line. I hung out with our running back Lance Ball too. We had a bunch of cool college guys I hung out with. I even spent time with some of the basketball players, like Mike Jones and DJ Strawberry, who was really popular, with his dad, Darryl Strawberry, playing baseball for the New York Mets and other teams. We would all go to DC every now and then, but we mostly spent our time on and around campus.

They had a lot of bars around College Park too, and my favorites to go to were called Bentley's and Cornerstone. They were all off of Route 1, right outside of DC.

I also used to go back to DC quite a bit, with Maryland being so close to home. I didn't try to stay around too long or hang out in the streets or anything like that. Really, I didn't even go outside much when I was back home in DC. I didn't want to get caught up in anything stupid. So, I mainly went home to check on my grandmother before heading back to school.

I remember bringing my brother Vontae onto campus with me a few times, showing him around the place, but I didn't do that too much because he was so young. I was eighteen to his fourteen. That age difference doesn't seem that big when you're growing up together, but once I went to high school and college, my brother was just too young for the people that I was spending time with. But he came on campus and sucked it all up.

My grades at Maryland were good enough to keep me alive with everything I wanted to do. We had to have, like, a 2.6 GPA to be eligible for football, and I did a little better than that, so I was able to keep playing with no worries. I chose criminal justice as my major because I thought about working for the FBI. So, I took all kinds of courses at Maryland, like forensics and other subjects that had to do with criminal justice. I was thinking I wanted to be in forensic science, the people who break down all the evidence in crimes.

I took several history courses as well. While studying criminal justice, they wanted you to know about some of the most well-known criminal cases in history to understand how everything works or breaks down in the most extreme cases. That's where forensics comes in, which is why I was so interested in it. I was fascinated by how guys can solve the craziest crimes. I don't remember anybody calling me a big, dumb jock or anything like that when I went to Maryland because I've always applied myself and went full throttle on everything I wanted to do. And that included learning things.

I actually changed my major from criminal justice to art studio and communications in my sophomore year because I saw a couple of my teammates taking those courses, and they were very intriguing to me. I thought it was pretty cool to watch them come up with art canvases and other artistic things. It was just calling my name to get involved myself. It was like the art world was just calling me. Then, when I turned pro, I found out that my biological grandfather had artistic skills. I never met him, but I had an uncle Floyd on that side of the family who once created a painting of a bear for my cousin Shamika's birthday that was really colorful, and they framed it. Man, I used to love that bear!

I was really impressed with the creation of that birthday gift, and my uncle Lloyd, my cousin's father, told me how good my grandfather was at drawing. I mean, he was really talented. Uncle Lloyd was fortunate enough to have a relationship with him, but the rest of us didn't. So, I always wondered about my grandfather and thought about his ability to draw and create different things when I became interested in art myself. I was still young at the time, but I remember that colorful bear vividly.

Instead of taking the rest of the criminal justice classes I would need for the major, I started taking classes in mass media, journalism, writing, and other arts. I ended up taking metal casting classes, sculpture, painting classes with drawings, and stuff like that.

In my junior year, I definitely felt like a campus celebrity; everyone wanted to take pictures with me. I got a little bit of that in my sophomore year too, but not at all in my freshman year. Nobody knew me then and I didn't do much, outside of what I had done at Dunbar in high school. But in my junior year, things definitely got a little bit crazy! One day I was walking into the stadium for my final home game against Boston College and the whole stadium was yelling, "One more year! One more year! One more year! One more year!"

They all knew I was going to leave for the pros after that junior year; the NFL Draft hype was that strong. What they didn't know was that I was on a mission to get to where I was trying to go. I was never bored at Maryland because we were always working. We had offseason winter workouts, spring drills, and, of course, the early summer camps. Our football workouts never ended at Maryland, and I never stopped working out on my own. I would never complain about getting stronger, faster, and bigger. That was the goal in college. We even had spring football games for the underclassmen.

They also moved us around frequently, from the dorms or for the different camps. They would have us somewhere for the summer. Then they'd put us somewhere else the next school year. I must have moved into a different building every year I was there. By my junior year, I lived in such a nice place, it was like going from a motel to a hotel. That's when Janel could come over more.

Even Coach Ray eased up on me that junior year. I guess I had morphed into a fully grown man, right there under his nose, while playing the position that came really easy to me. I became dominant, which was good! Coach Friedgen even told me he was thinking about me returning punts if I decided to come back for my senior year. He just wanted to get the ball in my hands as much as possible. I had done so well already that I didn't need to come back.

Now, I always knew that I was going to leave school early. That was my game plan. I just had to get out there on the field and get the opportunity to shine first. So, beginning in my sophomore year, I started exploring more information about what was needed to go pro and gaining my confidence. That sophomore season was a real confidence builder for me.

Once I learned what I could do on the field and in a game, I knew I was going to come back the next year and do even better. When I did that, things started to happen. I started getting really involved in the offense. That's when I *knew*, right then and there, that I would have a strong opportunity to leave school early on and go pro, based on the grade that the scouts gave me. I knew exactly what kind of effort I was going to need to get where I wanted to go.

I never really looked out for the pro scouts who were at the games, though. I was just happy to be in college and playing football. I wasn't worried about all that. I was just worried about playing the best ball that I could, while having fun out there on the field. I think I started hearing all the draft talk about mid-season. At first, they were saying I would be a *late* first-round pick. So, the hype was serious, but not as serious as it was about to get.

Believe it or not, I wasn't focused on all the NFL talk. I had my head locked in on the job at hand. When the season was over, I had to start thinking about my future. That's when I started thinking about the draft grades that the pro scouts were giving me. I was like, *Okay, I now have a first-round grade*, but when I heard that, I was thinking to myself, *I'm going to go a lot higher than that.* I just *knew* I was going to be a top ten pick.

I finished up my classes that junior year, but I didn't have enough credits to graduate. I figured I could come back to school and get that done later. At that time, I was ready to go through the process of declaring for the draft after a sit-down with our player development guy (PDG). So, what you do is talk with your PDG about what you're planning. He helps you with the process of declaring for the draft. It seemed like every individual school has their own PDG who works with the players specifically about going into the draft. They talk to each athlete about staying in school or going pro.

Our guy for player development was Kevin Glover. I went in to talk to him, and he already knew, or had an idea, that I could go pro that year. It was basically an easy conclusion with my draft grade being so high, but I still had to go through the process of seeing him and speaking with him, just in case I was on the draft bubble and would be better off with another year of college to strengthen my chances. That clearly wasn't the case with me. My first-round draft grade was rock solid. So, we made the decision to declare for the draft after my junior year.

Once that decision is made, the PDG will help you pull together everything you need to lock in your projection, or even do better, which included participating in the NFL Combine, where you do drills, running, jumping, catching, and all kinds of other stuff for all thirty-two NFL teams in Indianapolis.

The whole Combine experience was a real process for elevating your draft status with the pro scouts and the teams. When I first arrived, I remember meeting a lot of different coaches, but I focused on doing my best, and I kept listening to the Eminem song "Lose Yourself," because I related to what he was saying at the time, to just go for it all and lose yourself while trying to achieve your goals.

That song really locked in the moment that I was in, you know, just having one shot to prove yourself to the world, while defeating the odds that are stacked against you. But first you have to have the confidence in yourself to go for it. That song was all about achieving something greater than you've ever imagined. If you don't do it, *right now*, you may never do it. That's what Eminem was basically saying. Succeeding in life is about having that onetime urgency to go for it.

If that's the lifestyle you lead, of course. Because some people have jobs that are all about doing things with consistency for *years*, that may have nothing to do with one-shot deals. With sports and entertainment, it doesn't really matter how long you've been doing it. When you arrive at that next level of where you want to be, you have to go for it; nothing is guaranteed for you later. I could have gone back to school for my senior year and broken my leg or something crazy. That actually happened to guys. They even had college football player insurance for that. It was called Lloyd's of London, and I think they had amateur player insurance for basketball too. Many guys would just go pro unless they already knew in their minds that they wanted to come back and graduate first.

Going for it all was what I was thinking as I continued to listen to that Eminem song. I didn't view the Combine any other way. It was my one shot to do what I had to because I'd come too far to lose it all, to let that opportunity slip away. I wanted to change the narrative for myself, my family, and for those who looked up to me. So, for those few days that I was at the Combine, I prepared myself physically and mentally to put up some record-breaking numbers. I was going over it all in my mind before I even went out there to compete. I just pictured my performance in my head, over and over again, visualizing it.

I even told Norv Turner, who was the offensive coordinator with the San Francsico 49ers at the time, that I was going to run 4.3 seconds in the forty-yard dash at the Combine. I saw him out there in Indianapolis, and of course he didn't believe me. He laughed and said, "Good luck." I was dead serious when I said that. Sure enough, I went out and made it happen.

After I decided to declare, I sat down with my grandparents, Adaline and Lynwood, and told them my plans. They listened to me nicely and calmly; then they asked me, "Why would you want to do that?" For them, getting a chance to go to college on a scholarship to get an education while playing football was great. That was the goal. But I wanted more than that. They didn't understand how big professional football was. They had no idea how much guys were getting paid to play football in the NFL, or what the process was to get drafted into the league.

My grandparents just didn't understand what going to the pros was all about. My grandmother didn't even watch football, and my grandfather was a blue-collar working man who didn't have dreams about sports. He didn't know much about professional sports either. They surely didn't understand the amount of money that was at stake with my decision to join the NFL.

So, they were like, "Are you sure you want to leave school? Are you sure you want to do this?"

I told them, "Yeah." My mind was already made up. They just didn't understand what my bigger goals were. But I kept trying to explain it all to them.

I said, "I have an opportunity to make a lot of money." And I did. Being a first-round draft pick in the NFL is major! My grandparents were looking at me like I was making a big mistake. I hadn't really talked to them about me going pro before that. I had to do my work on the field first. You can't walk around talking about going pro if you don't get a chance to show what you can do on the field. So, it kind of caught my grandparents off guard.

That all happened in the early spring semester of 2006, after we ended the season in the fall semester in December of 2005, right before Christmas break. Once I declared to enter the draft, all these exciting things started happening. I had to get myself ready and fully prepared to enter into the draft mentally and physically. So, I went ahead and did all of the paperwork and started training for the Combine.

By the time all of that happens, everyone knows that you're going pro, so you start thinking about what teams may be considering picking you at your position. Once I did all that, and got prepared to start my training, I had to focus on securing an agent. It's relatively easy when everyone knows you've been graded as a first-round draft pick. They just start calling you.

There was a guy I knew already who became an agent, Melvin "Mel B" Bratton. He ended up representing me on my first contract, but I was only with him for two years. Mel B used to play in the league, and then he became an agent and hooked up with Zeke Sandhu. They partnered up in the business of representing young players, and my family really liked them when we all met up.

I ended up signing with them before they set me up in Arizona to train. I then headed out there by January of 2006 and started training while waiting for the NFL Combine. After that first two years of them representing me, I felt like I wanted something different. I had been talking with my boy Patrick Powell, who had become my business manager after college, and we had some other ideas about my career.

Mel B was definitely there for me when I needed to get started, though. I appreciated him for that. He met with my grandparents and my whole family over dinner, and everyone loved him. I think we all went to dinner at Busboys and Poets on Route 1, right down the street from the university. It was all agreed upon that I would sign with him, and then I showed up at the NFL Combine in Indianapolis that year and ran a 4.36 40-yard split. But they gave me an official 4.38. They didn't want to give me that 4.36 because it was too unbelievable. I think it was the fastest tight end 40 time in NFL Combine history.

After that, I really moved up the NFL Draft charts. I can't remember who first contacted me, but I know the NFL reached out. And it was *crazy!* They were looking at me as the best tight end in the business when it came to college football that year. They had me ranked in the top ten in all of college football. That landed me the invitation to New York's Radio City Music Hall, which I mentioned earlier.

Man, I was as excited as ever! I had been watching guys get drafted at Radio City Music Hall in New York for *years*! Who hadn't watched the NFL Draft who really wanted to play football? That's like a singer watching the Grammys, or an actor watching the Academy Awards. It inspires you to keep going for your own opportunity someday. We all turn on those events and watch, while rooting for whoever we feel is most talented and deserving. It's, like, the best of the best when you're on that level. That was what the NFL Draft was, and what I was being invited to.

Back in the early 2000s, they didn't have as many guys invited to the NFL Draft as they do now, though. You would only have five or ten guys invited back in those days. Everyone else would have a camera crew inside their house for their reactions. I was actually invited to be there with my family. I mean, you're talking about the top players in all of college football.

That was *crazy*! I wasn't coming from, like, USC, Florida, Michigan, or Ohio State. We're talking about coming from *Maryland*! I don't think it really hit me that way at the time. I didn't think about it like that until after the draft analysts kept talking about the more powerful football schools. You know, they have pre-draft shows that talk about the best players on the radar, and a lot of them were coming from the more football-dominant schools down South, in the Midwest, and out West. Those were the schools that got more football attention, never the East Coast schools—at least not for football. The East Coast schools got more clout in basketball. So, yeah, me cracking into that top draft level from Maryland that year was a big deal.

But you know, my grandparents still didn't get it. I don't think they believed me, really. My grandmother was looking at me like I was crazy. "You heading all the way up to New York for a football draft?" she asked me in a state of confusion.

It was nothing my grandmother would ever think about. Again, she didn't watch football unless I was playing, and that usually only happened *after* the games. However, once they realized that I was serious, they got all excited to go. Otis understood what was going on from the beginning. He was the only one who really watched and followed football like that.

The NFL Draft committee said they would pay for everything. So, when they asked me how many family members would want to come, I answered, "About eight."

"Not a problem," the NFL said. "We want all of your family members there so you can celebrate this big moment. You're a top draft choice, and we're going to make sure we take care of you."

My family started thinking we were going to have some steak and lobster and chicken and potato chips, all up in New York City. The NFL actually had a whole weekend planned for us. We rented the van to drive up to New York, and the next thing you know, we're in the middle of all these screaming and yelling fans, wearing team jerseys and mascot masks at Radio City Music Hall. And we all had a blast! They also had all the NFL commentators and sports media people all over the place with lights and cameras to cover it all. They had Al Michaels and Stuart Scott out there, covering and commentating, with a bunch of other football analysts.

I had taken draft trips to talk with the New York Jets, the San Francisco 49ers, and the Oakland Raiders. But you never really know who's going to pick you on draft night; teams can move around and go in different directions from what you thought they were going to do. It's not like you're the only player that they're evaluating. Things can change really quickly on draft night, depending on what other teams do.

We had all kinds of food at the table, and my family was enjoying it all—hamburgers, chicken, fruit, potato chips, and drinks—but I couldn't even eat that night. I was that nervous. I knew I was going to get picked, but you're sitting there waiting for your whole *life* to change because as soon as they call your name, you know you're going to be signing an NFL contract as a first-draft pick, which means you're going to make the most money of all the rookies, worth millions of dollars a year. So, I was just there waiting nervously for my phone to ring.

I remember watching the phone on the table next to some potato chips, as if it was locked in time, like a fossil. Then I got a call from Norv Turner at the draft, who was the offensive coordinator for the 49ers at the time, with Mike Nolan as the head coach. Norv got me on the phone, and he said to me, "Man, how you doing, buddy? It's snowing. We're taking you. We're taking you with the sixth pick."

That's how they had it set up: the team calls you and your phone starts ringing to let you know who it is that's drafting you before they announce it. When that phone rings, you already know who's next up to be drafted. So, Norv called me like that, and I looked up at the draft board for the next pick going to the San Francisco 49ers, and I just started crying.

We could all see that San Francisco was on the clock at number six, but I initially thought I was going at number four to the New York Jets, and with us being right there in New York City, they had plenty of fans out there that night. Instead, the Jets went with Ferguson Bickerstaff, an offensive lineman. He was a big-time dude that year. But man, I was happy to be drafted anywhere, especially at a place like San Francisco. They had a lot of football history and Super Bowl championships.

I remember the San Francisco 49ers fans started hooting and hollering after my name was called. Then I walked up onstage with my 49ers hat to shake Commissioner Roger Goodell's hand and get a San Francisco jersey. After that, they pulled me aside to do a draft night interview with the main network. After the main network interview, a ton of other interviews followed. Folks were pulling me in every direction to get in a word or two on what I had just achieved. The story was, I had just made history. My draft position that night would be locked in the books forever.

When I returned to our family seating area, I hugged all of my family members and felt so proud and appreciative. I mean, I was so happy, I didn't know what to do with myself. It was just a lot going on. The whole thing was a process. I even had a custom-made suit designed by this guy down in Atlanta. Somebody referred him to me, and I decided to let him go for it. The suit ended up being dark blue and black, and I wore a black, blue, and orange tie that just *popped*. I wanted to be different, you know. We accomplished just that.

Afterward, I had a bunch of businesspeople and opportunists pitching me all kinds of things to get involved in. It was just so much going on around draft time. It's, like, you're really caught up in a tidal wave where you're not expecting all of that water to flood you from everywhere.

I remember the price of the suit even surprised me. It ran me about three grand. But I got everything with it: some shiny black shoes, the tie, a dress shirt, and fancy cuff links. Everything came with it, for three thousand dollars total. And I paid for it with new money.

All of that didn't come from my agent either. I'll just say that the wrong people knew I was getting drafted that night. These guys knew how to get money, so they put me on their IOU list. I had a lot of new credit too. Credit cards and banks extended me credit for about one hundred grand. Man, I was twenty-two years old and hadn't ever used credit like that. My family didn't have the money for me to be using credit. You know you'll eventually have to pay that money back, and I didn't really have the ability to do that until I got drafted that night.

Even after I got drafted, I never had to pay back the money that people helped me out with during that transition period. I just see it now as another benefit of all the hard work I put in to be successful in football and to make it to the pros. You just create a lot of good karma through old-fashioned hard work, and that's what I was able to do.

Really, from the time I started making plays in my junior year, all the way up through draft night, that whole process was crazy. Once I was officially in the league, that's how people responded to it, coming from every direction. You would have people who made suits and custom-made clothes for big and muscular men. You had people who made fancy watches and jewelry. You had people who sold customized cars. You had people selling designer shoes and pushing apparel deals. I mean, just *anything* and *everything* that you could want or could ask for. People were coming from every direction to try to pitch and sell you something.

Because I went to Maryland, where Under Armour was created by Kevin Plank, a former Maryland football player, I got my first endorsement deal with them, right off the bat. That was, like, a no-brainer. His grandmother even lived in DC, like mine. The rumor was that he started making the first Under Armour gear right out of his grandmother's basement. So, I could relate to that. Definitely! He was close to his grandmother like I was with mine.

I remember we did a hot commercial for Under Armour Click Clack cleats. It was me, AJ Hawk out of Ohio State, who ended up going to Green Bay, and Julio Jones out of Alabama, who ended up going to Atlanta. We all shot the commercial out in Dallas, Texas. We had a lot of fun shooting that commercial, and it raised my national popularity. You know, more people would recognize me, and the cleats were hot. They came in all kinds of colors and styles.

My longtime girlfriend Janel from high school, she was still right there with me at Radio City Music Hall. She never really cared for money grubbing and gold digging. She cared about me. So, that was a special thing to have for your support, somebody who saw you go from the basement to the attic and out on the roof. She was wearing a black dress that night, right next to my dark blue, black, and orange. Janel looked so beautiful that night. She stole my breath away.

After I got drafted, I couldn't even head back home to DC with Janel and my family. The 49ers flew me right out to San Francisco the next day. As I said, I never graduated from Maryland. I had quite a few different types of credits from changing my major, but not enough to graduate. So, maybe I'll go back and do that one day. Maybe that'll be a new goal. Better late than never.

Chapter 6
I'm a 49er

THE SAN FRANCISCO 49ER BRASS FLEW ME OUT OF JOHN F. KENNEDY International Airport in New York the next day, right after the NFL Draft. I headed to the airport and was immediately on my way to the team. It was my first time flying first class too, so I was sitting nice and happy up front on the plane. It was a surreal moment in time for me, but I couldn't really feel it all yet. It was unraveling minute by minute. I was sitting there on the plane in my window seat, telling myself, *Wow! I'm on my way to San Francisco in first class.*

As soon as I landed on the other side, the 49ers had a security escort to pick me up from the airport and take me to wherever I needed to go, including my hotel. He was a middle-aged, white man who was designated to pick up the new players as they came in. So, he picked me up and drove me straight to the 49ers' football facility. I can't remember the escort's name, but he was a really nice guy.

I didn't even have a chance to go and put my things down at the hotel before meeting up with everyone at the 49ers' facility. I just remember walking into the bathroom—where the players' lockers were—and grabbing my San Franscico 49ers helmet and staring at my image in the mirror. I just couldn't believe it! It was a dream come true.

The first person I met when we arrived at the facility was head coach Mike Nolan. He was with Norv Turner, the offensive co-ordinator; Dr. John York, the owner; Pete Hoener, my tight end coach; and a few other 49ers staff members.

At the time, the 49ers hadn't built their new stadium yet, so the facility was pretty basic and not really up to par with the architecture and technology they had at some of the newer NFL facilities that we would visit during the season. One of the top ones was definitely the Dallas Cowboys. The Cowboys' facilities, either old or new, were always top-flight. I can say that right now: The Dallas Cowboys always had a great facility.

Now, don't get me wrong. The San Franscico facility looked nice to most people. Even to me, it was the nicest place I had seen at the time. Of course, I would go on to see a lot more nice facilities during the actual football season. But still, me flying out there to San Francsico after the draft was beautiful, it really was. One of the perks was that they had catered food for the players every day, with a chef cooking you special meals. You could order whatever you wanted to eat. I loved that too!

Actually, there were a lot of NFL facilities that were newer and nicer than the 49ers'. I wouldn't exactly say that San Francisco's facility was old school, but we didn't even have a cafeteria that first year. We all ate outside under a tent because the weather was always so nice out there. But I really wasn't worried about them not having a cafeteria. I was just happy to be drafted by the 49ers and being given an opportunity to do something that I had *dreamed* of doing.

However, let me add this: Once San Francisco upgraded to the new Levi's Stadium in Santa Clara, we definitely had a facility to brag about. You know, everything was upgraded to state-of-

Vernon at the tender age of four.
Credit: Vernon Davis Family Album.

non's grandmother Adaline
grandfather Lynwood in 2017.
dit: Vernon Davis Family Album.

Vernon enjoying family time with his mother Jackie sons Jianni and Valaughn, and his daughter Valleigh *Credit: Vernon Davis Family Album.*

Vernon pictured with his sisters Ebony, Veronica, and Christina, mother Jackie, and grandmother Adal *Credit: Vernon Davis Family Album.*

Vernon walking into a restaurant with his mom for Mother's Day 2017 in downtown Washington, DC. *Credit: Photo taken by a random stranger.*

Vernon with his beloved grandmother Adaline on her birthday. *Credit: Vernon Davis Family Album.*

Vernon doing a photo shoot in the neighborhood he grew up in with his children
for a clothing line that he had ownership in.
Credit: Vernon Davis.

Vernon pictured with his best friend Kal Ross and his children Valaughn, Valleigh, and Jianni at the premiere for the movie *The Ritual Killer* in Crystal City, VA., in 2023.
Credit: Jeff Gear Shift.

Vernon during his rookie years with the San Francisco 49ers. *Credit: Vernon Davis.*

Brothers or rivals? Vernon posing with his brother Vontae Davis who played cornerback for the Miami Dolphins, Indianapolis Colts, and Buffalo Bills.
Credit: Photo provided by Vernon Davis.

Vernon Davis and Thomas Mann on the set of Adam Sigal's *The Chariot*.
Credit: Olexiy Kryvych.

Vernon Davis and Bruce Willis in 2021 on the set of *A Day to Die*.
Credit: Michael Misetic of Overtime PR.

Vernon in the studio recording his debut rap album, *Showtime*, with fellow DC native and multi-platinum music producer Tone P. *Credit: Jacob Clark, STTP Media.*

Vernon Davis and Tone P on the set of the music video for "Bounce Like Dis." *Credit: Jacob Clark, STTP Media.*

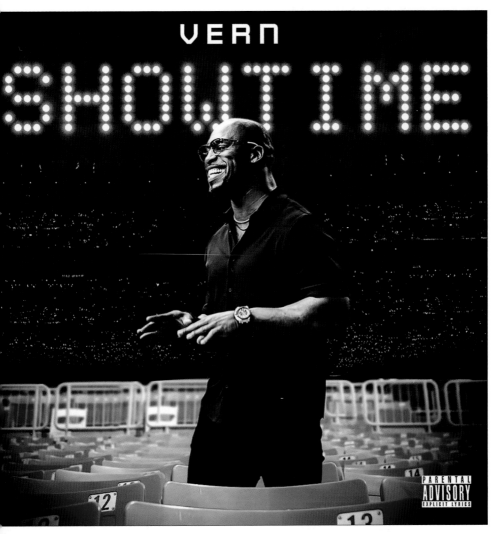

Vernon Davis dropped *Showtime* in the summer of 2023.
Credit: Jacob Clark, STTP Media.

Vernon Davis starred alongside Morgan Freeman in the 2023 action-thriller *The Ritual Killer*, directed by George Gallo. *Credit: Brock Morse.*

Vernon Davis and his business manager, Patrick Powell.
Credit: Michael Misetic.

Vernon's manager and partner, Henry Penzi, who helped catapult his acting career in 2021.
Credit: Vernon Davis.

Vernon Davis with his late friend and publicist Jeff Ballard at his LA apartment
before his appearance on *Dancing with the Stars.*
Credit: Lauren Vonderpool.

Vernon Davis and Alex Smith
at the Washington Redskins gala
in Washington DC in 2018.
Credit: Vernon Davis.

ernon shaking hands with
rmer president Barack Obama
ter one of his campaigns in
in Francisco in 2013.
edit: Photo provided by
rnon Davis.

Vernon Davis with George Galo, Morgan Freeman and Cole Hauser in Jackson, Mississippi doing some film promotion for *The Ritual Killer*.
Credit: Vernon Davis.

After an epic career as a professional NFL player, Vernon Davis has reinvented himself
as a true renaissance man.
Credit: Manfred Bauman

. Vernon Davis is ready for whatever action and exciting projects may come his way in the next chapters of his life.
Credit: Manfred Bauman.

the-art technology and design then. But every team is upgrading nowadays. Teams upgrade their facilities every few years to stay up with the times. San Francisco was one of the latest to do it. You also get a Super Bowl when you upgrade your facility. So, now we've got a Super Bowl coming to Las Vegas with their Allegiant Stadium. That's going to be crazy!

I remember when I arrived in San Francisco; it was just me out there, you know, because I was the first draft pick. So, I got a chance to meet with everyone individually. My teammate, Manny Lawson, was the second guy they drafted that year, and I saw him later in the next couple of days. But again, because I was picked before him, they flew me out there to meet up with the organization and staff first and gave me a nice room at the Marriott.

I didn't even have a change of clothes with me for all of that, but by then I had some money in my pocket and a line of credit. So, I had money to buy new clothes if I needed to. I wasn't that worried about it. For the most part, the team leadership wanted to meet me and help me get situated and acclimated to being a San Francisco 49er, while living out there in the Bay Area.

The process of getting acclimated started with my first walk around the facility to meet everyone, while getting fitted for the equipment—my helmet, cleats, shoulder pads, *everything*. They didn't really talk about the 49ers' history, the older guys who were on the team already. They just spoke to me about the program and what they were trying to do. Then we went over some scenarios and plays to explain how they were going to integrate me into the offense.

The word they kept using to describe me was that I was a *mismatch*, and they were trying to use that to the team's advantage. Coach Nolan wanted to use me all over the place. He said I could create a lot of decisions to make as a mismatch for poor defenders. That's when teams used a lot of linebackers to cover tight ends. What teams would do is put their fastest linebacker on a tight end to cover him.

Opposing teams tried to do that with me initially, but no one really knew everything I could do, or what I was going to bring to the table until I started playing and showcasing it all. You know what I'm saying? You can talk the talk, but you have to be able to walk the walk for it to mean anything. So, a discussion was started on how certain teams and linebackers were going to drop back and try to cover me and things of that nature.

What happened was, once I got acclimated to the offense, and the NFL in general, I started creating havoc in the league for coverage linebackers who were used to much slower tight ends that they could easily run with. Most linebackers couldn't run with me. I was too fast for them. After a while, teams decided they had no choice but to try to cover me with a safety. Then they found out that the safeties couldn't cover me either. A lot of the bigger safeties were not agile enough to cover me. Then teams tried to cover me with a nickelback, which is like a hybrid between a safety and a corner. Realistically speaking, the nickelbacks were too small to cover me. Whenever I thought about a team trying to do that, it got me real excited in San Francisco for what we could do. That was after the opposing teams realized that few linebackers or safeties could cover me one-on-one. Teams figured that out *fast*.

On that first visit, we were more in San Jose than in San Franscisco. I remember the Marriott Hotel in Santa Clara was right down the road from San Jose, and it was right next to California's Great America amusement park. The park was so close to the hotel, you could literally walk to it. I figured it was the host hotel for people who stayed at the park from out of town.

I had flown out to San Francisco before I was actually drafted, and even made a visit to Oakland. That's how it goes when you're being looked at before the draft, especially if you're a top prospect. You fly out to meet four or five teams that are really interested in you. They'll fly you out to get a chance to sit you down with the coaching staff, meet everyone, and show you the city. You know, they show you the lay of the land.

So, it was great for me to be back again in the Bay Area for a longer and more meaningful visit. I was pretty much at the facility for all five days that I was out there after being drafted. I was learning everything I needed to know to get started. That's what I was there for. I didn't really go anywhere else. I was just busy talking to my family and getting acclimated. Man, I was just overjoyed about the whole process, and I called back home to my family a lot.

Even though I was just happy to be there, I also felt overwhelmed by it all. It was all such a new experience for me. That second visit was very different from the first because now I was actually drafted. For me, that meant a commitment and a responsibility to play up to their expectations and standards. It was a big deal just being able to take it all in while meeting the people who I needed to meet.

They had me sign my contract with my agent as soon as I got out there, like the very first day. So, my agent, Mel B. Bratton, flew out there as well, to be with me for my contract reading and signing. They included in the contract exactly how they were going to allocate the money to us. So, I was all good. The team owner, Dr. York, Coach Nolan, Coach Turner, the general manager, and my agent were all there. What I heard most was, "Congratulations, gentlemen! This is well deserved!"

That was the key word of my draft selection, *deserved*. Everybody kept telling me how well-deserved my pick was. "You deserve it, Vernon! Congratulations! We can't wait to get you out there on the field. We're excited about what you're going to do to help this team win games."

After those first five days of hanging out in Northern California with the 49ers staff at the facility, I flew back home to DC. I was back home for about two weeks. I had to get myself situated to move to California, and by that time I was already thinking about a house. As soon as I got my first official check from the San Francisco 49ers, the first thing I did was buy a house.

I bought that very first house out in Silver Spring, Maryland, for my grandmother to move into with the family. You know, I wanted to get my grandmother and my family out of DC. But we never sold the house in the Petworth area. So, what happened was, my grandmother moved out there to Silver Spring for a little bit, but then she missed DC and didn't like being out there in Maryland. So, eventually, she moved back. I think she was just used to being in the District for all those years. Moving out to Maryland was too different for her.

I started using the Silver Spring, Maryland, house myself later on, during the offseason. I'm glad my grandmother didn't want to leave or sell the house we grew up in back in DC because that house is now worth in the upper six figures. I just felt that buying a house was the first stage of me becoming a man who does what he's supposed to do.

Before I settled into that first house in Silver Spring, I used to stay in the same Maryland apartment building during the offseason that I shared with roommates when I was still at the university. It was the same apartment building I had in my College Park days at the University of Maryland. And what I did was just keep the lease going with my college guys and any family members who were still there. So, I went back home and started packing up my clothes, preparing to check out of my apartment, while trying to get my car shipped out to California, because I had a new car that I needed to get out there. I had bought a Cadillac Escalade and put Lamborghini doors on it, that opened *up* instead of *out*.

Man, it's like, every time I think about that vehicle, I think about the time I left it with this guy named Raymond, who had an auto dealership, because I needed somewhere to store the car while I flew in and out of town from California, or wherever. But I didn't want to leave the car at the Maryland apartment building. And this guy Raymond ended up vanishing with my vehicle and I never got it back or saw him again. That was a big lesson learned. But how was I supposed to know a legitimate businessman would just disappear like that over a custom truck? I guess he loved it as much as I did.

I remember I was even thinking about selling my vehicle because I was traveling so much without it. I wasn't sure what I wanted to do with it yet. Then, when I flew back home to get it this one time, Raymond was gone. I couldn't find him anywhere. I mean, he just took off, man, and he took my Escalade with him. That broke my heart. It wasn't like I couldn't buy a new one. It was the principle of being able to trust people with your valuable things. That incident became a valuable lesson for me.

Ironically, I ended up running into Raymond just a few years ago. He came up to me and said, "Vernon, how have things been going?"

I had spotted him at this event I was at in DC. I saw him when I first walked in. I didn't say anything to him, though, you know what I mean? After he took off with my truck like that, I wanted to see what he would say to me. So, I saw him and knew who he was, but I just stayed where I was, to see how things were going to play out.

When he eventually walked up to me and said something, I said, "Oh, hey, how are you doing, Raymond?" as if I hadn't seen him at all.

"Yeah, I'm good, man," he said. Then he added, "You know, I gotta make you whole again, right?"

He was talking about stealing my Escalade SUV the way he

had, and he was *guilty*. However, I just decided to blow it off. Like I said, it was a big lesson for me to learn early on in my career.

So, I told him, "Nah, man, you don't owe me anything. You taught me a lesson with that. You taught me something I'll never forget," I reiterated to him. "You taught me a valuable lesson, man, something that most people won't get a chance to experience. I appreciate you, brother. You don't owe me anything."

I actually said that to him because I took for granted that I could trust this man without really knowing him or thinking about having a real relationship with him. I just *assumed* that he would do right by me. And he hadn't. So, I learned not to ever *assume* anything like that again, especially when there's money or valuable property and assets involved. I learned that lesson early and the hard way. Stay on your business no matter what. Don't *ever* assume anything about anyone. Make sure you *know* who you're doing business with or leaving your property with. You feel me? That's a very important lesson to learn when you start making nice money.

By that time, I wasn't even mad about it anymore. I couldn't be. It was my own fault, so I took it all in stride. You know, that just goes back to having "the fruitage of the spirit" that's mentioned in God's Holy Word, the Bible. By that time in my life and career, I had peace, love, joy, patience and kindness in my heart. So, I wasn't worried about anything like that breaking me from when I was younger. I had already made way more money than that truck was worth, and it was no longer a big deal to me. But the lesson was a big deal. And I learned it.

Another important lesson I've learned is that if your soul and spirit are in alignment, and you have the fruitage of the spirit within you, you'll know exactly what to say and what to do when you're challenged by the unexpected things that happen in life. Make no mistake: You *will* be challenged at some point in time. We all are. That's just life.

Of course, I was initially *pissed* over losing my truck like that. I never even got a chance to transport it out there to California with me, where I rented a home in an area called Santana Row. I lived in California by myself until I could get things situated for Janel to move out there with me. I even furnished the place all by myself.

Janel would come out there to see me from time to time, but she didn't make any immediate plans to move out there with me. But I definitely got acclimated to the place. I was living by myself that first year, but my boys Patrick Powell and Todd Stewart used to come out there all the time to see me. They were, like, my regulars. Patrick was flying out there to Cali like every other week.

Todd went to the University of Maryland too, but he graduated before our time. He also had a younger brother, Tyrone Stewart, who I knew really well. We all had a lot of mutual friends, all from being around the University of Maryland.

Todd liked to go out and party. He was like my inside man to all of the best parties in DC and Maryland. I would call him up whenever I wanted to go out to figure out where we wanted to go. Of course, when Todd and Patrick started flying out to California to visit me out there, I had to take them to some of the best parties they had out on the West Coast so they could experience how different their parties were from our parties back home. I remember around that same time, Patrick had graduated from Maryland and he had started going to school for philosophy up at UMass (University of Massachusetts) in Boston. You know, Patrick was really a smart guy, that's why he ended up becoming one of my most trusted friends and business partners.

Back on the football field, San Francisco had about fifteen to twenty rookies on the team that year of 2006, including me, outside linebacker Manny Lawson, wide receiver Brandon Williams, and Delanie Walker, who played wide receiver in college. The 49ers brought Delanie in with the idea of converting him into a tight end with me. He was a really funny guy too. We used to hang out a lot. Delanie Walker was my guy.

Then we had this guy named Juicy. I don't remember what his real name was, but we called him Juicy because he had a Jheri curl, and he would work out and get everything wet with his hair. This dude thought he was the smoothest man alive. He really did. I believe he was from Chicago, but I'm not certain. We also had a guy named Anthony "Spice" Adams, who was a real energetic guy who played defensive tackle and got into blogging, social media, and hosting television shows and stuff. I think he does some acting now too. Both of these guys were vets with interesting lives. We had a lot of fun getting to know all of the guys at practice.

I remember, during one of my first team workouts, I walked in and saw the veteran players. These were the professional San Francisco guys I had seen on TV and knew of already. I was excited to be their teammate. One of these veteran guys was Frank Gore, the legendary running back. He was one of the first players I recognized and greeted. In fact, Frank Gore became one of my best friends.

Practice back then wasn't like it is now, when the league implemented a bunch of rules to stop coaches and teams from pushing guys too hard. We still got really physical back in the year 2006. Oh, we were absolutely physical. However, we still weren't allowed to tackle each other unless we were playing an actual game or having a scrimmage. Even then, we had to keep one another up instead of a full tackle.

I was competing with all of the guys right off the bat at practice because I was strong, physical, and big. So, I was able to compete however they wanted to. I just had to learn the techniques at the professional level. That's when I discovered that in the NFL, it didn't really matter how big you were or how strong you were, you still had to use your mind. That was the most important part, because you had to be really strategic when going up against guys at the professional level.

Try to imagine me as a rookie going up against Warren Sapp from Tampa Bay. Well, I actually did have to go up against Warren Sapp during my rookie year in the preseason, when he played for the Oakland Raiders. It was tough, but I held my own against him because I was ready for it. That was also an older Warren Sapp than when he played his prime years in Tampa for the Buccaneers.

I'll never forget the first time we scrimmaged them. That Oakland Raiders game was my very first professional scrimmage in the NFL. I even have a picture of it in the house. I was catching a pass over against Michael Huff, who was a first-round draft pick for the Raiders that year, who was selected right after me. I mean, *literally*, I went number six and he went number seven. So, I went up against Warren Sapp and had to block him on the line, and then ran out to catch a pass against Michael Huff, who played strong safety. Man, that was next-level competition that got me excited. I kept telling myself, *Time out! Is this really happening?*

You know, I wanted to respect those guys, but I also wanted them to respect *me*. So, that first meeting meant more to me than just a first game. I wanted to go *hard* for it. I went so hard at Warren Sapp that day that he told me, "Man, I'm gon' to dump you on your head if you grab me like that again. You hear me?"

I didn't respond to that. I didn't say anything. It was one hard shot and nothing to brag about it. So, I was like, "Next play, next whistle."

I just wanted him to know I wasn't playing around with him. They still beat us that day. We weren't really a good team yet. The organization was trying to rebuild, and we actually got into fights and scuffles at our own practices. I'm talking about among my teammates in San Francisco. When we had live hitting between the offense and the defense, temperatures raised and we got into fights every day.

When I first came in, we had a guy on the team named Parys Haralson, who played outside linebacker out of Tennessee. He was drafted behind me that same year in the fifth round, and we had to square up against each other all the time for blocking drills. And man, we used to go *at it*, because he liked to practice hard too.

Parys would come off the snap and be very disruptive and aggressive. He was really difficult to deal with. He had an incredible burst of energy and drive to keep going. Originally from Mississippi, he was recruited to play ball in the next state over for the Tennessee Volunteers instead of Ole Miss (University of Mississippi) or Mississippi State. Parys was big, too, like six-three and 255 pounds, and was still quick as a cat. We used to fight at practice all the time, and neither one of us wanted to lose.

I remember there was a video released of us fighting. One time I even threw his helmet, and the coach tried to calm me down because he swung at me after I blocked him. So, I swung right back at him, and I snatched his helmet off his head and threw it up in the air.

"Vernon, come back here!" the coach yelled at me.

But I was so teed off at Parys that I ignored the coach and snapped again at my teammate: "Fuck you! If you hit me, I'ma hit you back."

I was raised that way in DC, where a grown man was expected to stand his ground. I would need to change my ways as a professional, though. That lesson was yet to come. And rest in peace to my teammate, Parys. He died like three years ago in his sleep. Nobody really knew what he died from. I think it was an aneurysm.

The team had been struggling before I got there, so we were still rebuilding in my early days in San Francisco. That's why they were able to draft me at number six to begin with. I didn't even start in a lot of the games that season. It was more off and on, as I continued to learn the plays and the system. We had a tight end named Eric Johnson in front of me on the depth chart, and we were going back and forth like a committee kind of thing that first year. It wasn't really a good season either. I think our record was 7–9, which wasn't that bad, but it wasn't good enough to make the playoffs.

I didn't really mind playing behind Eric Johnson that rookie year. They had brought me in to start, but he was already there, and I was supposed to be backing him up. I only ended up with three touchdowns that rookie season, but I didn't really touch the ball that much either. I can tell you one thing, though, my first catch and rookie touchdown with the 49ers was historical.

In the first game of my professional career, our quarterback, Alex Smith, hit me in perfect stride for a thirty-one-yard touchdown against the Arizona Cardinals. The only reason I remember it is because everyone still talks about it. I scored two more touchdowns that rookie year, one against Green Bay that was fifty-two yards with a long run, and the last one was just eight yards against Seattle.

I really only had, like, twenty receptions that first year and two- to three-hundred yards. But it didn't matter to me because I was in the league, and I knew I would get better and be featured more in the offense. I also got a minor leg injury in that first year that made me miss some games. So, I had to be patient and wait my turn, just like I did in high school and in college.

Janel got pregnant after that first year in the league as well, and that was unexpected for us, but it was better that it happened then instead of while we were still in high school or when I was in college. That would've been a problem. Fortunately, Janel was on birth control for quite some time while we were dating. I'll talk more about that in a minute.

I have to say this book writing process has forced me to remember a lot of things that I was no longer thinking about. It's making me reflect on some of the significant and memorable things that happened to me back then. It's a good thing we have Wikipedia and the Internet now, to list and document so many of these occurrences. It's possible that I may even forget things now, due to being hit in the head while playing football for so many years. Maybe my grandmother had it right not to watch it.

I remember hanging out in the Bay Area a large part of the time on my off days and during the weekends. I used to go out in San Francisco, especially after the games; they were right near the city. We played about fifteen minutes away from downtown. I used to hang out with my teammates in the city. Sometimes, we'd hang out so late that I would just go straight to practice the next morning. We would get a driver or just catch a ride with one of my teammates from the game and then head back to practice.

In fact, if I knew I was going out after the game, I'd just get a driver to pick me up, and he'd be waiting for me out in the parking lot. That allowed us all to drink and not worry about driving back home afterward. We were really responsible when it came to the drinking-and-driving thing. In those days, a driver typically cost us about fifty bucks an hour, and I'd probably be out for five or six hours a night after the game. I may have done that about four or five times during the season.

The culture out there in Northern California was totally different from DC. They were all about the hyphy movement, where people dance with their heads moving from side to side while making facial expressions. It reminded me of some of the creative energy of Black Greek fraternity and sorority dancing. I mean, the lingo and everything else they believed in was very different from what I was used to in the DMV. Instead of go-go music and East Coast rap, they listened to a lot of Bay Area music from their own local artists.

With the hyphy movement, everybody was cool out there. The great thing I loved about the city is that they embraced you, all the boys from the city, the 'hood guys, the dope boys, *everybody*. They just embraced us. They looked out for us and never really wished us harm. I can't say that about other cities and cultures. I could never feel that way in DC because I know too much about the people there.

They also had more of a mixed crowd out there than we had in DC and Maryland. But that also depended on where you were going. If you were going to a hip-hop spot, the majority of the crowd was going to be Black folks. Even when it was a majority Black crowd, more of the women seemed to be mixed, like part Black, part white, part Asian, or part Hispanic. It was just different out there, and you always seemed to have more ethnicities hanging out together, even if it was at a Black club. I mean, they had mixed girls out there everywhere. I pretty much had to learn how to relate to the difference in cultures.

At the end of each season in San Franciso, we would all go in for our exit meetings, check out with the coaches, do our physicals, turn in all of our equipment, and pack up all of our garments, like everything you had in your locker, and put it all in a box to take home. At your exit meetings, the coaches would give a recap of the season and what all you needed to work on to get better for the next season.

During my exit meeting, Coach Hoener said, "Vernon, you had a terrific year, son! You gave us something to grow on. Now we're going to build off of it and try to put this thing together for next year. And we're going to be okay."

I said, "Yeah, I know it. I believe we're gonna come back way stronger, Coach."

You know, I was always upbeat and positive about the future. I said, "I know it wasn't meant for us this year, but next year is going to be our year, Coach. I *know it*! I can *feel it*! And I appreciate everything you're trying to teach me."

My teammates were like, "Great job, Vernon! We'll see you again for next season," you know, because we were all from different cities and everybody didn't hang out like that in the off-season.

Chapter 7
"I'm Pregnant"

ONCE WE WENT THROUGH OUR EXIT INTERVIEWS AT THE END OF that first season in San Francisco in 2006, I was on the first plane smoking back home to DC for the offseason. No disrespect to the Bay Area, but at that time, while I was still young and fresh out of college, I still liked hanging out in DC, especially without any homework, team rules, or school assignments to work on. So, I rented out a place in Maryland for about two thousand dollars a month, and I would go and hang out with the guys I went to college with.

I never really hung out with a lot of different guys. It would pretty much be my same crew. When it came to the parties, my man Dontae Hogan was the guy. Dontae and I got close enough to be brothers. He was a slightly older, light-skinned dude who always had my back when we went out. I knew him from DC even before I went to Maryland. Dontae was around back in my Dunbar High School days, but he didn't play football. He was a hype man at a lot of the DC parties. He made sure I made it back home safe every time. Dontae would always drive my car or ride in the passenger seat when I drove to make sure I was on

VERNON DAVIS

point. From being well-known at the DC parties, of course, he knew a lot of people.

My other party man, Todd Stewart, was like my brother too. Every time people saw me, Todd would be somewhere close by. Of course, Patrick Powell, who I *did* play college football with, has been one of my main guys for more than twenty years now. Those are the guys I hung out with while renting my Maryland apartment or a town house for three to five months a year. Sometimes, I would rent places fully furnished.

The attention I got back home once I went pro was crazy. I remember I used to go to all of the Marc Barnes parties when I was in town. His parties were like the top events in DC for a long time. I used to go to all of his spots.

Ironically, with all the time I was spending back at home in DC, I still wasn't close to my mom back then. Instead, I would spend time with my grandmother, Adaline, and my grandfather, Lynwood. I even hung out with Vontae, Otis, and the rest of the family, but my mother remained an issue for me. I just wasn't close to her. I was still hurt by everything that happened in my youth, and my family understood that. They saw all the bad stuff that was happening, and nothing had really changed.

My grandmother was still holding everything together in the family with my grandfather backing her up. Otis was still doing his thing, and my mother continued scrambling around to do her thing and find more drugs, while still lying to us about it. We just never knew when she was telling us the truth, so we tended to doubt everything she said.

My grandmother was still not watching live football games, but at least she let the family fill her in on what was going on in my first professional season. My younger brothers, Vontae and Michael, were both watching me, though. They started getting ideas about following in my footsteps, especially Vontae, because he had already followed me to Dunbar Senior High School in DC, and the team had won several more Turkey Bowls.

Vontae ended up being rated as one of the top thirty cornerback recruits in the country, and he also stood out in track-and-field, like I did. He chose to go to school away from home at Illinois, instead of Maryland, Virginia, or Michigan State, who all wanted him. Vontae watched my games on TV and said, "Duke, you look good out there." He still called me Duke after my father. In fact, my whole family still called me Duke. He followed that up with, "Duke, in that Green Bay game, you did good on that big run for the touchdown. And I knew they wasn't gon' catch you. You were out of there!"

Michael had to put in his two cents as well. "Duke, how you make that play against that boy in the Seattle game? He couldn't handle you, Duke. He couldn't handle you. He wasn't ready for it!"

My brothers just kept on talking that talk and were proud of me. They talked football with me every chance they got, and they knew to work on their games to get there because they saw me working and knew what they needed to do. I had hired my own trainer by that time, Michael Flowers, who I trained with in DC. In fact, Michael Flowers started training all of the biggest stars out of DC. He would take us back out to Maryland to train. I was actually the first player he started working with.

So, I kicked it all off. Before me, there weren't that many big football names that came out of DC. I became one of the biggest players ever to come out of DC for football. We had Josh Cribbs, who made it to the league before me, and then after me, of course, we had my brother, Vontae, who Michael Flowers trained. He also trained Arrelious Benn, who played wide receiver at Dunbar and got drafted by Tampa Bay in 2010. Another player he trained was D'Qwell Jackson, who played linebacker at Maryland with me and was drafted by the Cleveland Browns. Currently, Michael trains the Diggs brothers: Stefon Diggs, who plays wide receiver for the Buffalo Bills, and Trevon Diggs, who plays cornerback for the Dallas Cowboys. They both came out of the

DMV area too, with Stefon going to Maryland and Trevon going to Alabama.

I remember I would stay home in the DMV area for Christmas and for all the other holidays to train with Michael. I would head to where he trained people at Gold's Gym up in Silver Spring, Maryland, to work out for two hours a day, three days a week. We would then go to different places around DC and Maryland to do our field work. We even had spots in Silver Spring where we would go. Then we would run the hills at Coolidge High School in DC. So, my work never let up. I knew I had a second season coming with the 49ers when I would be expected to do more, and I wanted to be ready for it.

When our early training camps rolled around for the next season, we had some new standout guys on the team. Each year, new guys would get drafted to the team, along with free agents being signed. One guy who really stood out to me in that second year was Patrick Willis, a linebacker. The team drafted him out of Ole Miss at number eleven the year after me, and he was a real *beast*. He tackled everything that moved. But as everybody knows, he had these problems with his feet and his cleats. He would have at least thirty different pair of cleats stashed in his locker, trying to figure out which ones might work best for him. That happened every season and at every training camp.

After a while, I really felt sorry for him, especially when he retired early because of the issues with his feet. Patrick was a really good player and a real stand-up guy. When he first joined the team, we knew we had someone with Parys Haralson to really help us out on defense and get us more wins. But his feet just wouldn't let him play without hurting himself.

I was starting regularly in that second year, but I missed a lot of the season due to a sprained right knee that happened in practice. Then I got hit in that same knee when Troy Polamalu tackled me in a game against Pittsburgh. It was our third game that season, and I was having a crazy game too. I felt ready to go off on Pittsburgh that game. I remember catching a pass and Troy hit me low. He's a lot shorter and smaller than me, so a lot of those guys go low to get you down when you're bigger. It was a thirty-five- to forty-yard pass into the Red Zone to set us up for a score. I think it might have been a seam route, with me cutting straight up the field. Troy just ran right up on my legs and scooped me, and I ended up injuring my medial collateral ligament (MCL). The good thing about it was that I didn't need surgery. It was only a *sprained* MCL. Thank God!

When it happened, I got up and was a little wobbly in my stance. The medical staff walked me straight off the field, onto the track, and into the training room. Then they escorted me to the back to get an X-ray of my leg. After a couple of minutes went by, they told me exactly what it was. That was only the first part of the process. The next day I had to get an MRI because that shows everything. An X-ray can only give you a standard look, like a general image of what's going on. But when you take an MRI, it shows you every little nook and cranny, so the medical staff can really study what's going on, and I got lucky that it wasn't an ACL (anterior cruciate ligament).

The MCL is a lot safer than an ACL. An ACL is the exterior part of your leg, whereas the MCL is more inside, which doesn't require surgery. So, the medical staff and doctors told me I was looking at five or six weeks for recovery.

Then Troy got my number somehow and called me up to apologize. He said, "I'm sorry, man. I didn't mean to hurt you. I was moving fast and just playing football." He was really sincere about it and a good sport. I thought he was a real stand-up guy for calling me like that. I didn't even know him at the time. But I ended up being out again in my second season after missing several games in my first year, when I suffered a leg injury in practice. My teammate, Moran Norris, who played fullback, accidentally ran up on the side of my leg on a play. He was behind me while blocking for the running back, and he ran right smack into me. It was a freak accident, and I ended with my first injury as we prepared to play the Philadelphia Eagles, where I got hit in that same spot and cracked my fibula, which was nonsurgical. I ended up missing four weeks of my rookie season because of that injury.

After both of those injuries, I recovered during the season and went right back to playing football. Coach Norv Turner was the creative mind behind the offense those first two years, and he really began to design plays for me in the second year. I felt like he was the most creative offensive mind I ever worked with.

When I came back from the injury, the team medical staff and coaches started me off slowly. I have to admit that I was nervous and playing timidly. I was just nervous to get back out there because I didn't want to reinjure my knee. Once I settled back into playing hard and fast, I ended up with fifty-two receptions and over five hundred yards that second year, which was double what I had the first season. I averaged nearly ten yards a catch that second year, which wasn't bad at all.

My individual game got better, but our team got worse, going backwards that year with only, like, five wins and eleven losses.

That was also the year that Janel got pregnant. She was flying out to stay with me in California and it just happened. She was about four months along in the pregnancy before she got up the courage to tell me.

"I got something to tell you," she said to me.

"What is it?" I asked her.

She kind of whispered, "I'm pregnant."

It sounded to me like she was ashamed of it. We had been dating for years at that point, but we still didn't plan on a pregnancy. We didn't even talk about having kids. I mean, we would've planned on it eventually, but it just snuck up on us kind of fast. Again, we had been dating for quite a while and everyone knew one another in our families, so it wasn't like a *shock*, or something we couldn't handle. I obviously had the money to provide for children at that point, and I had succeeded in my goal of making it to the NFL. So, having a family with Janel seemed like the next thing that should've happened for me anyway.

We didn't immediately jump the gun to get married, though. I said, "It's okay. It's all right. I think it's a great opportunity for us. This is amazing. Let's embark on it. Let's be great parents and a couple who raises our kids the best way we can."

She was happy about that. She replied, "I can't wait. You're right. I'm excited."

Then I asked her, "Did you tell your mom yet? Or anybody else?"

"No. I was waiting to tell you first. I wanted to tell you," she answered.

When we told her mother, she immediately told us how she felt. "Congratulations! I hope it's a girl."

In retrospect, it wasn't like I was a stranger. I mean, I used to live with her family in high school, but we didn't force ourselves to get married after that. We just kept living together like we'd been doing. From time to time, we did talk about getting married, but for me, I knew that the divorce rate in the NFL was extra-high. I didn't want to be a part of that. I always told myself that I was going to get married after I was done playing professionally. That was my mindset at the time.

I clearly remember watching Jerry Rice going through a divorce when I first got to San Francisco. It was all over the news: JERRY RICE LEAVES JACKIE. And, you know, he had his kids, and I knew everything that was going on because I know the family really well. Jerry Rice and I had the same personal assistant, Sasha Taylor. I met her when I first got out there and was looking for an assistant to help me with my transition. So, the 49ers recommended that I work with Sasha.

That's how I got to know Jerry Rice and his family. I had a

front-row seat to seeing his divorce play out, and it seemed like everybody else around me was getting a divorce. I thought to myself, *I don't want to be a part of that.* I just wanted to make sure I did things the right way and maybe get married after I was done playing ball, because it seemed like the NFL lifestyle put a lot of stress on marriages.

I believe, as young men with popularity and money, you can get so tempted, like everywhere you go. Guys just get tempted and have so much going on that it's hard to keep your marriage in order. It's tough when you put yourself in a situation like that because there's just so many opportunities to get your hands on different things that can cause conflicts.

So, I told Janel what my issues were with marriage, and she said, "I understand." She had been with me for so long, she knew I wasn't out there running around on her. The woman had faith in me. I just didn't want the extra stress of marriage at that time.

Of course, every woman wants to get married, but Janel never spazzed out on me about it. She wasn't doing all of that. We ended up having our first son at the end of September 2007, right as the season was underway for my second year. We named him Jianni Lenon Davis. We had two more children after that, a girl named Valleigh Davis in 2009, and another boy named Valaughn Davis in 2014.

When we had our first son, Janel had been flying back and forth to California to see me, but once we had more kids, we decided I needed to be around them more as a father, so she moved out to California with me. Even then, she continued to fly back and forth to see her family in DC and during the off-season. So, she never really stayed with me full-time during the season. They would be with me once a month during the season, and during the offseason I was with them full time. Janel spent a lot of time away from me and by herself, even while she was pregnant and raising our children. Then she found a spot back in DC for whenever I went back, but we never ended up getting married. Instead, we grew apart and became disengaged with each other.

Initially, I was upset about it because I was expecting for us to be together for a long time. We had basically grown up together. You know what I mean? So, it was very upsetting to separate, not to be able to go the distance together. The truth is, Janel wanted to get married before I was comfortable with it. I just didn't want to *be* married at that time. It seemed like marriage could bring out the *worst* in some people, especially if you're around professional athletes and all of the money that tempted people. I just didn't want all of that in my life. Janel and I had a good relationship without being married.

I can't remember why Jerry Rice got a divorce. And I never asked him. Because I had conflicted feelings about marrying Janel, I discussed the idea of marriage with my pastor, John Erwin, who I met in California after I started going to his church and consulting with him. Pastor Erwin gave me advice on everything, including marriage.

At the end of the day, a pastor shouldn't judge anybody. You can't make someone do something they don't want to do. A pastor's job is only to give advice where it's needed. He basically told me to take it all one day at a time. You know, when done right, marriage is a beautiful thing. Janel is a truly beautiful woman who has always been supportive of me, which I will be eternally grateful for. She bore some beautiful kids with me. So, it was only right that I made the strides to work in the direction of us getting married. That's how I thought about it back then.

One piece of advice that Pastor Erwin gave me that I'll never forget is when he said to me, "Vernon, just because you're not married doesn't mean I can judge you. Only God can judge you." Then he added, "Life is not about where we are at the moment, it's about what we're going to be in the future." At the time that I sought his counsel, I took it to mean, maybe it wasn't meant for me to be married on that day, or that year.

Pastor Erwin strongly believed that I was going to *get* married. He just didn't know *when.* He couldn't give me a definitive answer on that. But he did say, "Just because you're not married don't make you a bad person. You're a wonderful human being. God doesn't judge us based on what we do or how we do it. He judges us based upon our hearts. That's what He does. He looks deep inside our hearts to see if there's good or bad."

Essentially, that's what Pastor Erwin said to me about the subject of me getting married. God looks at your heart and *He* knows exactly what you're thinking and what your intentions are. But for me, at that time in my life, I just had to continue staying true to my word, staying close to God, putting *Him* first, and having faith that He will direct my path.

Now I know that it wasn't up to me to direct my own path to marriage. I strongly believe that *God* will direct me down the correct path at the right time. I just have to trust the process. That's what Pastor Erwin said for me to do—trust in the process. I had several of these kinds of conversations with him throughout my time in San Francisco because I was thinking about proposing to Janel and getting married to her. Unfortunately, we were never able to settle in on the ebb and flow of our relationship. So, by the time I finally proposed to her around 2016, our relationship was already coming to an end.

I still think marriage is a beautiful thing. I really do. I think everybody should get married. Marriage is meant to be for two people who love each other and want to spend the rest of their lives together. I mean, it's really a wonderful thing. It just hasn't happened for *me* yet. I just haven't felt comfortable enough to take this life-changing step. To this day, Pastor Erwin continues to advise me about it.

So, yeah, I had all three of my children with Janel. I couldn't ask for a better mother for my children. After being together for sixteen years, we finally got engaged. Sadly, before we could go through with the plans for marriage, we decided to separate. It was heartbreaking that we never got a chance to follow through on getting married. We just weren't clicking in the relationship anymore. It seemed like, after having three kids together, she was who she was and I was going in another direction with my career.

I would say in general that when Janel first met me in DC, I didn't really have good people skills. Back in my high school days, I wasn't going to go up to somebody and just talk to them. If I was standing at the elevators, I wasn't going to start a conversation. So, I had to work on myself and get prepared to become a more sociable adult because I didn't grow up that way.

I grew up in a predominantly Black neighborhood, where we didn't really trust people we didn't know. As you can imagine, being a Black boy in the inner city, I'm not about to have a random conversation with a stranger. I had to really work on myself to get there, and by the time Janel and I had grown apart, I was already there, where I was much better at meeting and talking to people. I just had to get myself on point.

By my third year in San Francisco, I already had two losing seasons, and I was ready to win and contribute more to the team in 2008. Alex Smith had been my quarterback for all three years. In fact, the team had drafted Smith as the number one pick in 2005, the year before they drafted me, and Norv Turner as the offensive coordinator. Mike Singletary, from the famous Chicago Bears team—the legendary 46-defense—was on board as the linebackers' coach for Parys Haralson and Patrick Willis.

Well, in that third year, as I continued to get better, with more catches, more yards, and more touchdowns, that's when my game started to explode on the pro level. I was getting better and better every week. That's also the year when I had the incident with Coach Singletary, when he sent me to the locker room in the middle of the game. That happened in 2008, during a divisional rivalry game against the Seattle Seahawks. We were already having a bad season that third year. We were still struggling, but the 49ers owners were thinking we were on our way up. But it never happened with Coach Nolan. Norv Turner was no longer the offensive coordinator by my third year. We had a new guy, Mike Martz, who had taken over the role.

When Coach Mike Nolan got fired in the middle of the season, it was the week before that game against Seattle, and everyone thought Martz would get the interim coaching job because he was the offensive coordinator. Singletary wasn't even a coordinator at the time, but the 49ers organization liked his tough approach to coaching, and they honored the great job he had done with our linebackers, particularly with Patrick Willis, who won the Defensive Rookie of the Year (D-ROY) award after his first season in 2007.

So, we played Seattle again. We had to play them twice a year within our division with the Arizona Cardinals and the St. Louis Rams. We had beaten Seattle the first game in a high-scoring shoot-out that September, 33–30 or something like that. I remember Patrick Willis had, like, an eighty-yard interception return for a touchdown that game. We were feeling good about our chances to beat them again, even though we had a losing record. Seattle hadn't been winning that many games that year either.

I was playing pretty well that year before the infamous Seattle game. I wasn't doing as well as I had the second year, but there was a new offensive coordinator and a new coach involved, so we all had to learn the new systems and plays. Sometimes you have to go through those initial learning curves of a new system. You know, it's not automatic. Everyone has to get on the same page, so you can't really rush things. Because then you'll have guys who know the plays and guys who don't, which would destroy the overall team chemistry.

PLAYING BALL

By the time we played that infamous Seattle game in October, Alex Smith had been banged up as quarterback and he was put on the injured reserve list. So, our backup quarterback, Shaun Hill, got to start. Ironically, Shaun Hill had come out of the University of Maryland when I was still playing high school ball at Dunbar. He went undrafted and was bouncing around the league for a while as a backup. He even played quarterback for a team over in Europe before he ended up with us in San Francisco.

In our second Seattle game that season, I ran out to catch a short pass and got tackled by the Seattle Seahawks safety, Brian Russell. I don't remember what he said, but whatever it was, I got mad and slapped him in the facemask for it. We got a fifteen-yard penalty that wiped away the play and our field position.

I have to admit that I was just being silly, man. I didn't really mean anything by it. I guess I had reverted back to DC in my mind and had caught that boy out on Georgia Avenue in the Petworth area, you know. But I didn't have to do that. He was supposed to tackle me, I just didn't like the extra comments he made. I thought it was disrespectful.

That can happen when you play a few years in the league; you start feeling privileged as a veteran player. I don't think I liked the fact that we were losing so many games either. Losing definitely added to my frustrations that year. We were already down in that game, like, 27–10 in the third quarter, and I was just *pissed* from all of the losing.

Well, when I got over to the sideline, Coach Mike Singletary just went *off!* I knew my behavior was unacceptable, so I was already saying "Sorry" as I walked off the field while looking at him.

Coach Singletary looked back at me and said, "Go take a shower."

At first, I thought I heard him wrong. I thought to myself, *Did he mean to say that to me?* We had a whole quarter left to play in the game. We had more that we could do to still win, with plenty

133

of time left, and I wasn't quitting. I was frustrated, but I still wanted to play football. Playing ball on a football field had become my *life*, you know. So, I still wanted to play. But you can't play if you're back in the shower in the locker room.

After Coach told me to go to the showers, I said, "Huh? What do you mean, Coach?"

He told me again, with those hard eyes of his through his glasses, "I said, go take a shower."

Right then and there, I was thinking that I probably couldn't beat him. Mike Singletary was known to be a little crazy. Everybody on the team felt that way. You didn't want to mess with him. So, I put my head down and walked off the field toward the locker rooms. When I got inside, I stripped down out of my uniform and took a shower while the game was still going on. The whole time, I was thinking, *This is crazy!* But that's what he asked me to do, and he said it to me *twice*, so he really meant it.

I got home after the game—which we lost to Seattle 34–13— and I was sitting in front of the TV watching the sports news of the game with Janel sitting right beside me. By that time, my son Jianni was a one-year-old. He was there with us too that night. That's when we first saw the story of Coach Mike Singletary going off on me at the team press conference after the game, and I was in *shock*. I just couldn't believe he had done that to me. I felt like he could've said all of that to me in the locker room instead of airing it in front of the media for the whole world to see.

I looked over at Janel with our son with us and said, "Wow! This is *crazy!*"

Chapter 8
Coach Said What?

BY THAT THIRD YEAR IN THE NFL WITH THE SAN FRANSCICO 49ERS, everyone on the team knew not to mess with me. I had a reputation by then as a guy who could go crazy on you. They already knew my size, speed, and strength. If anyone on the team had something disrespectful to say to me, I was going to be ready to fight.

My attitude had gotten that bad. One time—in my second year with the team—I even got into a fight with offensive lineman Larry Allen. Now, Larry Allen was a big boy and a respected veteran player at six-three and 325 pounds, with a mean streak of his own from Los Angeles, California. I mean, Larry Allen looked like he hung out with the Bloods and Crips out there in LA.

Admittedly, I was a little nervous, not knowing what to expect from him. Would our fight continue past the football field and spill into something more serious? I wasn't sure, but I was feeling really uneasy about finding out. Basically, the way the disrespect started, Larry Allen was telling me to buy him certain things when I was a rookie. He used to make me go buy him Louis XIII Cognac, which was *expensive*. He used to make me buy him that all the time. Every time he saw me, he'd always want me to buy him something. It got to the point where I felt like he was specifically looking for *me* to do that. After my rookie year had passed and I was in my second year, he was still treating me like I was a rookie.

On this particular day in training camp, during my second season, I went offside for a penalty against the offense at practice, and he yelled at me, "Stay onside, motherfucker!"

Man, I just blew up. I was sick and tired of taking his crap. I wasn't a rookie anymore. So, I said, "Nah, *you* stay onside, motherfucker!" as strongly as he said it to me.

Then he looked at me and asked, "What'd you say?"

I repeated myself. "I said, *you* stay onside, motherfucker!"

Then our teammates and coaches stepped in.

"All right, all right, Vernon. Get your head back in the game. The play is over, all right?"

After that, the coach took me out. So, I walked over to the sideline, and I spotted Larry walking in my direction with his right fist balled up. Man, I was ready to swallow my damn tongue! I had no idea what to expect from that dude. I mean, this was a big, strong man walking over to try to take my head off.

He walked over to me and shouted, "Hey, look at me!"

"Yeah, what's up?" I responded. I was still nervous about it, but if a real fight between us was on, then it was *on* at that point. I wasn't going to run away from him. Everybody was right there with us.

When he got close enough, I swung at him in slow motion. Then he grabbed my hand, and I grabbed him right back. From there, he couldn't do anything with me. I locked his arm up with mine and wouldn't let him go. It doesn't matter how strong somebody is when you're trying to protect yourself. So, I held on to him for dear life, and I was ready to fight him if I had to. You know, I had to protect myself at all costs.

That's when everybody ran over to break us up, but I was still worried about Larry Allen getting loose and using his strength on me. You know what I'm saying? They were trying to break up the fight, but I was still trying to protect myself. The truth is I was still scared. But I was also tired of him trying to play me like a flute. I was two years into the league and I wasn't a fucking rookie anymore! All I wanted from Larry Allen was a little respect. It didn't help matters that I had a chip on my shoulder.

So, I told him, "Come on, man, respect me." You know, we were still San Fransico 49er teammates.

But Larry wasn't having it. He said, "No!" as our teammates continued to break us up. After a while the situation cooled off. We still had practice for our upcoming game that day.

Once we made it through that unfortunate incident, Larry was cool with me and started treating me like the man I was. That all happened in training camp before the 2007 season. Larry Allen and I became friends after that. From that point on, he respected me and never did anything else to rile me up.

But yeah, Larry Allen was big and strong and mean, and he used to walk into our team meeting rooms, looking for anybody who was in his seat all the time. As soon as they saw Larry coming, they would get up and move. He used to come into the team meetings wearing a basketball jersey, while showing off those python arms of his. It seemed to me like he was doing all that on purpose. That's all he wore, basketball jerseys with Nike Air Force 1s on his feet. Then he'd have a toothpick in his mouth, while rocking shorts like it was always summertime. He had the whole California look going on, like Suge Knight from Death Row Records. That's what Larry Allen reminded me of, that whole West Coast craziness. So, everybody kept asking me, "You got into a fight with *him*?"

"Bro, I had to protect myself," I said in my defense.

In disbelief, my teammates made a point of telling me, "Bro, do you realize what you just did? You got that *juice*, now, bro. You just got into a fight with Larry Allen. He could have *killed* you!"

Larry was much older than us at that time too. He had already played eleven years in the league and had won a Super Bowl with Dallas.

I remember him telling me, "I have nephews your size."

With his slow drawl and accent, he sounded just like one of those California boys from the movies, as if he was about to stick up a 7-Eleven at the corner.

Give me all your sodas! I'm thirsty!

They even had a report in the *Mercury News* about our skirmish:

> *Tight end Vernon Davis and guard Larry Allen brawled on the sideline and had to be pulled apart by 49ers teammates and coaches in the midst of an intrasquad scrimmage that drew about 4,000 fans to the team's practice facility Saturday.*
>
> *Davis and Allen got into the scrape, which was largely out of view from the fans, after the first team offense failed to score against the second-team defense during a twelve-play possession. Neither Larry Allen nor Vernon Davis was made available after the practice.**

It's funny because Coach Mike Singletary had no problems with Larry. He went on to become a Hall of Fame lineman for the Dallas Cowboys. I hope I can join him one day in the Hall with the 49ers. But we'll see. Ironically, the strongest man football reports have me listed behind Larry Allen now as the third strongest man who ever played in the NFL, with Larry first and Andrew Billings, a defensive tackle for the Chicago Bears, second.

So, when I got into that situation in Seattle in 2008, no one said anything to me on the bench, in the locker room, or on the

*Dennis Georgatos, "Davis, Allen get into brawl." *The Mercury News*, August 4, 2007.

plane ride home. I had no idea what Coach Singletary had said about me until I saw the whole press conference on TV. And man, let me tell you, I know Coach Mike Singletary's rant by heart now.

I was sitting there at home on the sofa with Janel, watching Coach Singletary pop off at me on national TV. He said, "I will not tolerate players that think it's about *them* when it's about the *team*. And we cannot make decisions that cost the team, and then come off the field like it's nonchalant. I'm from the old-school, and I believe this. I would rather play with ten players and get penalized all the way until we gotta do something else, than play with eleven when I know that person is not sold out to be a part of this team. It is more about *them*, than it is about the *team*. Cannot play with them. Cannot win with them. Cannot coach with them. Can't do it!"

He continued his rant by saying, "I want *winners*! I want people that want to *win*!"

I know that speech now like the back of my hand. I was sitting there on my sofa with Janel and my son, Jianni, and I was thinking, *How could he do that? That's horrible. I can't believe he would do that.* Man, I was so frustrated. Actually, I was *livid!* I just couldn't *take it.* He had just thrown me under the bus on national television. That was awful! But like I said, I didn't think I could beat him in a fight, so what was I going to do? He was the coach.

That was the moment when everything turned around for me. Once I saw Coach do that at the press conference, I had an epiphany moment: *Wow, this guy is really serious.* I just sat there with Janel, shaking my head, watching it all on television, and thinking, *Man, is this dude out of his mind or what?*

Everybody was confused and trying to figure out why Coach would throw me under the bus like that. I was one of the best players on the team. Janel thought he was wrong too, and immediately said he needed to be fired. But of course she's going to say that and be on my side. At that time, I think running back

Frank Gore was one of the only teammates I could talk to about it. Frank Gore was always my guy.

So, I called Frank up and asked him, "Did you see what Coach did to me, man?"

Frank was quick to answer. "Man, I know. I know, dawg. But, like, you just gotta listen to him, bro. It's all good. But he shouldn't have done that, man. He shouldn't have done that."

On Mondays, depending on what we wanted to do that week, we'd normally have off, and then come in on Tuesday. Or we could take Tuesday off and come in on Monday. However, if you got injured in the game, you would have to come in for mandatory treatment, even if the team was off. I wasn't off that Monday because Coach Singletary called me into the office. And I wasn't injured. He just wanted to have a sit-down talk with me.

I showed up at the facility and walked into his office. He looked at me and I looked at him.

"Have a seat, son," he said.

I sat down in front of him, still livid from the way he laid me out in the press conference after the game.

"What's up, Coach?" I responded to him. I was curious to see what he had to say.

"What you need to be is a leader," he said to me, point-blank. "But you go out there and you slap my man in the face and get us a penalty."

"Coach, he said something to me," I responded in my defense. "I was just trying to . . . You know, he was talking crazy, Coach. He was talking crazy."

Coach looked at me calmly and shook his head. "Son, it's not about *you*. It's about the *team*," he said. "I can't play with nobody like that."

It sounded like he was going to cut me or have me traded to another team or something. I didn't know what to think. It all happened so fast that I started to panic. My heart started racing and everything. I could feel my heart in my chest. I loved being with the 49ers.

Then he said, "Do you know why I sent you to the locker room?"

"No, Coach," I answered.

He said, "You have to do better or find another team because we can't tolerate self-centered players."

In near desperation, I asked him, "What do you want me to do, man? I'm just trying to help . . . us to win." And I broke down and started crying. I mean, I had worked my whole life to be a professional football player, and I had landed on one of the best football organizations in the league, and I had just screwed it all up for myself. So, understandably, I was very emotional about it.

Coach saw that and softened up a bit. He understood that I had a good heart and just needed some tough love and discipline to straighten up my attitude.

Coach said, "Son, you can be *great* if you change your attitude and put the team *first*. You can be the best to ever do it. I really believe that because your talent is undeniable."

He paused and continued, "You got everything it takes to be the best. But it starts up *here*," Coach said, pointing to his head. "If you want to be *great*, you have to be a *leader*. You've got to listen to me, son. That's what we brought you here to do, to be a *leader*. And you can do it."

I was still crying, just trying to figure everything out and hoping that he wouldn't cut me or do something else drastic, like benching me for half the year or something crazy. But then Coach started crying with me. It was an emotional man's moment for both of us because I had worked so hard to get there, and Coach knew that. I just didn't want to mess things up.

So, he got up, wiped away his tears, hugged me, and said, "I love you, son. And when you come back in here this week, do you think you can be a leader?"

I nodded to him and said, "Of course. I got it."

The coach wanted me to be a team leader, and that was it. I didn't have a *choice* if I wanted to remain a 49er under Coach Mike Singletary. That was how he wanted me to be. After that one-on-one meeting in his office, the rest is history. I became a whole different player. Sometimes you need a kick in the ass like that to shake up what you've been doing that hasn't been working. And it's how you respond to that shake-up that will either make you or break you. That San Franscisco 49ers shake-up from Coach Singletary made me a much better player, a better teammate, and, most importantly, a better man.

After my heartfelt conversation with Coach, everybody started calling me and talking about the press conference. My family, fellow San Francisco teammates, guys I went to Maryland with, friends from back home in DC—they all wanted to know the scoop. The sports and TV networks must have shown that video of Coach Mike Singletary's rant, blasting me at the news conference, like a thousand times. I think it went viral on social media back then. My 49ers teammates started killing me with it in the locker room.

"'It is more about *them* than it is about the *team*,'" my teammates teased me. "'Cannot play with them. Cannot win with them. Cannot coach with them. Can't do it!

"'I want *winners*! I want guys who *want* to win!'"

In actuality, Coach's rant put me in a better place mentally, where my teammates were able to loosen up and joke with me more than the previous years, when I wouldn't go for that. You know, to be an effective leader, at some point, guys need to be able to talk to you and feel who you really are. They need to be able to relate to you. I hadn't really given my guys a chance to do that. So, the rant from the coach kind of forced me to put my guard down a little. You know what I mean? I became able to laugh it off.

So, I came back to practice that Wednesday, looked at the

tape of the game, and went back to working out. We practiced that Wednesday, Thursday, Friday, and then Saturday. I think we had off that week with a bye, so we got a chance to do a lot of walk-throughs before our next game to really get ready for it. And man, let me tell you, I came out a different player that next game. My attitude went from focusing on myself to focusing on the team, and that's all I thought about during our second game against the Arizona Cardinals. We had lost the first one to Arizona to open up the season, but we had a big second game against them. However, we still lost in a close one.

The score was something like 29–24. But the highlight of the game was when Shaun Hill threw me a touchdown pass in the end zone, where I had to leap over a defender to catch it. It was a crazy play, man, and crazy game! That play was like one of those cereal box commercials for Wheaties. It was *pandemonium* inside the stadium! But again, we still lost the game. However, what made the difference for me was how I had changed my whole football life and attitude. I think I had about six or seven receptions that game.

After the close loss, Coach Singletary looked at me. Then he tapped me on the shoulder and said, "I told you so. Just keep going."

It wasn't even about the loss anymore. It was all about *learning*. Despite the loss, that Arizona game became a standout teaching moment for me because that was the game where I finally turned the corner *mentally*, which is just as important—or maybe more important—than the *physical* game. That's what Coach was trying to tell me all along. And I finally got it.

After that close loss to the Arizona Cardinals, we went on a winning streak, but we had already lost seven games that year. So, even though we started to win at the end of the season, our record ended up being 7–9 again, with no playoff run like in my first year. I actually had fewer targets on the offense we ran with

Norv Turner as the offensive coordinator. We had a lot of turn-over at the quarterback position with injuries. But Shaun Hill played his butt off!

To top off the season, I think I had thirty-one receptions and more than three-hundred-fiftysomething yards, with only a couple of touchdowns that year. But it was about *more* than just my stats. I was blocking better, playing harder, and I had a much better teamwork attitude. Obviously, we were still struggling to win enough games. Nevertheless, we had *hope* for the following year. But hell, you *always* have hope for the next year. That's normal for every team. Realistically, though, it's tough trying to build a winning football team in the NFL.

Once I made it to my fourth year in the league in 2009, I was still on the team with the San Francisco 49ers, when Coach Mike Singletary was named as the head coach instead of an interim. That's the year I became a grown-ass man and a dominant player. In fact, before the season even started, I went back home to DC in the offseason and worked out like a *maniac* to get ready for it with a new, team-first attitude.

Man, I lit up the league like you wouldn't *believe* in that fourth year. It was the best statistical year I ever had in my *career*, in high school, college, or the pros. I had 78 receptions, 965 yards, and 13 touchdowns. That tied the all-time record for touchdowns by a tight end in a season. I also made the NFL Pro Bowl that year, along with Frank Gore, defensive end Justin Smith, Patrick Willis—again—and we had a punter named Andy Lee who made the Pro Bowl as well. Andy made the Pro Bowl the first time in 2007, my second season, when he was breaking records for punting that year.

Once again, we missed the playoffs with an 8–8 record, with another new coach, Jimmy Raye, as our offensive coordinator. He was a Black man from Fayetteville, North Carolina, who had played professional football back in the late 1960s, before he started coaching with a lot of different teams, including colleges. That first year with him, they made sure to get the ball to me a lot more, and we got off to a hot start with, like, a 3–1 record to begin the season. Then we went downhill from there. It was an up-and-down season for the rest of the fall and winter, when we just missed the playoffs by a couple of games.

For some reason, we just couldn't pull it all together to be more than average. There we were again, looking forward to the next season with Coach Singletary and Coach Raye. It was a news flash when they fired Coach Singletary at the end of the 2010 season. The whole league had a great deal of respect for Mike Singletary as a player, as a coach, and as a man. I just remember the San Francisco ownership saying they had decided to part ways.

I called Coach after hearing the news and said, "Coach, I appreciate everything you've done for me, man. I really appreciate it. We'll miss you."

And Mike Singletary—the man—coached me one last time when he said, "Son, I'm proud of you. Keep going. Keep becoming the player that I knew you could always be."

By that third year of having Mike Singletary on our staff as a coach, we all loved him. He was a tough guy, but he told you the truth and got you prepared to play your best football. We just couldn't pull it together for enough wins under his leadership. We had great experiences with him, though. In time, he had earned all of our respect. So, we players just spoke about the experiences we all had with him. He was definitely a different kind of man. And, after he was gone, we kept saying to ourselves, "Coach Singletary is gone. We gon' miss him."

We had some interesting years with him, too. For instance, one year Coach made us all go to the harbor and just sit there to listen to the water. That's all we did. I guess he wanted us to be in tune with nature. He was just *different* in that way. Every time we went to meet in his office, or around the 49ers facility, he had a different way about him, with out-of-the-box ideas. Mike was an old-school coach, and there was nothing wrong with that. So, the memories we all had of him ended up being some great ones. Some people thought his ideas were weird and crazy. As for me, I just thought they were different.

Another memory that stands out in my mind is a speech he made before a game. Coach came in with an axe and a piece of wood. During our team meeting, he started chopping the wood with his axe. He was chopping the wood to illustrate an analogy for us, that we should keep going and chopping away at the season.

"This is what we gotta do. We gotta keep chopping away at it," he said to us.

Some players were looking around and smiling, but you couldn't really laugh because he was serious, and you didn't want to make him feel like you were laughing at him. Of course, everybody talked about it afterward.

I remember Coach would look at us in the distance with his binoculars just to see who was walking through the drills instead of running or jogging. The position coaches would be out on the field working with us at practice, and Coach would be back in his office looking at us through his binoculars and saying, "Who's walking?"

He didn't like us walking around at practice *at all*. We couldn't ever walk around him. We couldn't even walk when we moved from one workstation to the next. We had to *jog* instead. You know what I mean? Coach didn't even want you walking to get *water*.

A lot of stuff became funny after the fact. I mean, everybody thought it was crazy that he would watch us from his office with his binoculars like a drill sergeant in the army. But to his defense, he just liked to see everybody jogging. So, for Coach Singletary, our team walk-throughs should have been called "jog-throughs" instead. He wanted us to be in constant movement, so we could have that same kind of stamina and energy during a tough, long game. In the end, it didn't equate to more wins or enough to make the playoffs again, though.

Sadly, during our final year with Coach Singletary, we went back to being 5–12, and they fired him, along with our offensive coordinator, Coach Raye. By that time, we'd already had four different offensive coordinators in five years. You don't have any consistency when you do that. We were constantly having to start over, while learning new plays and new offensive terminology.

Then we got Coach Jim Harbaugh out of Stanford in my sixth season with the team, in 2011. Stanford was right there in the Bay Area, so the ownership and a lot of fans were already familiar with him. We also drafted quarterback Colin Kaepernick that year in the second round.

I was on a new contract by then. That was about the only good thing that happened after my fifth season in 2010. I was re-signed to a $37-million extension of five years, with $23 million guaranteed, which made me the highest paid tight end in the league at the time. And man, that was a dream come *true*. It was just what I had told my grandmother and grandfather before I left college. I was about to make a lot of money for my family. But I still had to watch myself to make sure I didn't give it all away.

Chapter 9
Winning Time in Foot-ball and Business

I HAVEN'T TALKED ABOUT IT YET, BUT I STARTED TO SPREAD MY EN-trepreneurial wings a bit by doing art shows in the Bay Area while I was a 49er. I opened up an art gallery in San Jose, California. What I did was form the Vernon Davis Foundation for the Arts, with the objective of giving local artists an opportunity to showcase their work. I opened up the gallery and set it up in such a way that half of the proceeds went back to the foundation and the remaining half was designated for the kids who were creating the art. I displayed the work of local artists, specifically children and young adults. In addition to promoting the arts through my art gallery, I also bought a couple of Jamba Juice franchises in San Jose.

I had heard about the tennis stars Venus and Serena Williams owning Jamba Juice franchises, and I actually ended up meeting the CEO, James White, at the time. We formed a cooperative relationship with him, and the next thing you know, I opened up my own shop and later added another one. However, I didn't own the real estate the stores were on; I rented that. I bought my first Jamba Juice store for $100,000, and that baby brought in a million dollars the first year, before taxes. So, I got excited and bought four more of them in California. Unfortunately, they had to be shut down because of COVID. I wasn't interested in losing a bunch of money to keep them open until COVID was over. Nobody had any idea when that would end, and the company understood. COVID was a real back breaker for many businesses.

I also thought of bringing the Jamba Juice business to DC. The company gave me franchising rights to the DMV territory in case I wanted to do something in the District, Maryland, Northern Virginia, and other places on the East Coast. The one thing you have to be careful about is the weather. When it's cold outside at the beginning of the year, the sales drop drastically. That scared me about bringing the franchise to the DMV; it gets a lot colder on the East Coast than it does out West. Around that same time, I met up with the Williams sisters and cultivated a relationship with them. They became business friends of mine through the Jamba Juice connection. I kind of looked up to them and was impressed by what they were doing in business and with their brands.

I was living out in California, and I wanted to have something to invest in to make it seem more like home to me. When we negotiated the deal for the Jamba Juice franchises, the company allowed me to put my name on the store. So, it was Vernon Davis Jamba Juice. My boy Patrick Powell was working under my business manager at the time, a guy by the name of Amadou Tall. I met him through a mutual teammate of mine, Dashon Goldson, who played defensive back and safety. I think Dashon is coaching now. Amadou was representing him at the time, and I agreed to have a meeting with the agent. It wasn't what anyone *said* about him representing me, but what I *felt* from our meeting.

Amadou came right over to my house in San Jose, and he presented me with more of what I needed at the time. I saw a lot in him that I could work with. He was sharp, very intelligent, and he knew what he was talking about. The guy just knew what he was doing. So, I felt in my heart and mind that he was the best man for the job. He was the best person for me to work with when it came to my new business. Amadou ended up teaching Patrick everything he knows about the sports management business. After I parted ways with Amadou later on in my career, Patrick was there to step right in for me. But Amadou did the Jamba Juice deal. We really worked it strategically.

I also got involved with a company called Fantex, where people could invest in my football career as a stock. Basically, I sold like 10 percent of my current and future brand income as stock that investors could buy into. That's 10 percent of my $37 million contract, or $3.7 million to invest in, and as my value went up, the stock value did also. The company did the deal with me, giving me $4 million upfront for an opportunity for them to earn from my football career and the increased value of my future brand.

From that point on, I started getting involved in many different ways to increase the value of the opportunities that playing football had given to me, and the popularity of being involved in professional sports in general. Basically, the more I did with my brand and the better I played football, which was how people earned when my overall value went up. The company even called my stock VNDSL, which was an acronym for, V as in Victor, N as in Nancy, D as in dog, S, L. I even had my own ticker in the stock exchange, and the more the valuation of the VNDSL increased, the more my stock would go up. That included landing any new endorsement deals.

Creating new deals was actually the main part of my value. At the time, Fantex was responsible for bringing me new deals because the more I got, the more income they received, and the more my stock rose for those who invested in me. It was as simple as that.

PLAYING BALL

I got involved with the Fantex company around 2013, which was another big year of football for me. I caught another thirteen touchdowns with Colin Kaepernick as my quarterback. That was coming off our Super Bowl run with Coach Jim Harbaugh in the 2012 season. In fact, our Super Bowl game against Baltimore happened early in 2013, so my value was really high as a player and a brand at that time. I was catching a lot of touchdowns and racking up a lot of catches and yards at crucial times in the playoffs, and even in the Super Bowl.

The whole turnaround of winning for our 49ers team started with the hiring of Coach Jim Harbaugh in 2011. That was my sixth season with the team and in the league. As soon as Coach Harbaugh was introduced to the team, you could feel his energy right away. He had a charismatic way about him that gave you confidence immediately. The whole team could feel it. He had a lot of personality too. We just knew we were on to something.

Everything that Coach Harbaugh implemented was spot-on. I mean, we had a lot of the same guys on the team; the only thing missing was someone like Jim Harbaugh to lead us and help turn things around. With his simple formula, he was able to get the guys to rally behind him and start winning some football games.

His approach was totally different from all the other coaches I'd worked with while I was out in San Francisco. It was his ability to lock in on the details and the players to piece together exactly what we needed from the coaching staff, the offense, the defense, and even the special teams. Jim Harbaugh was big on holding everyone accountable, just like he was still coaching college. So, no one got a pass just because they were veterans in the league. Everybody had to show up and show out. I felt that was a great way of approaching a team concept that was *spot-on*. He was very personable too.

I remember the first time I met him. I walked up to him and said, "Hey, Coach, how are you doing?"

He replied, "Hey, good to meet you, Vernon. We're excited to be able to get to work with you. We're going to do some fun stuff around here."

"Yeah? Well, I'm excited to hear it, Coach. I can't wait, man. It's an honor to have you. I look forward to working with you," I answered back.

Harbaugh was very upbeat and particular about how we practiced, the workouts we did, the offense and defensive schemes, the players, and everything he wanted to accomplish with our team. As a result of his demeanor and strategy, we started winning right away. We ended up with a 13–3 record in his coaching staff's first year and nearly went to the Super Bowl. I remember we clinched the NFC West—the National Football Conference Western Division—and a high playoff seed that year, with a final win against the St. Louis Rams at the end of the season. I think it may have been the last game.

Alex Smith was healthy all season long that year and played every game. I was healthy and played every game too, and I had, like, six or seven touchdowns and about 800 yards receiving. Our main strength that year was defense. Coach Harbaugh took what Coach Mike Singletary started and turned our defense into a top unit against the run.

We had like, *seven* Pro Bowl guys on our defense that year, with all four linebackers—Patrick Willis, NaVorro Bowman, Aldon Smith, and Ahmad Brooks—Justin Smith at defensive tackle, and Donte Whitner and my guy Dashon Goldson at safeties. I think our 49ers defense broke records that year, with teams not being able to run the ball on us, which made the game one-dimensional. Once we knew your team had to pass on us, we could focus on getting to your quarterback.

It was a recipe for winning football games that Jim Harbaugh believed in: make your opponent one-dimensional and control the game from there. We still ran *and* passed the ball. You know, we still had Frank Gore, who was a Pro Bowl running back;

Michael Crabtree, Ted Ginn Jr., me, and Alex Smith could run a little bit too. Coach Harbaugh liked to use a bunch of power plays and physicality to win games. So, we were a physical team that really started with Coach Singletary.

However, we still lost in the NFC Championship game that year in overtime to the New York Giants, 20–17, with a backup punt returner who fumbled the ball after a punt. The Giants ended up winning the Super Bowl that season, 21–17 for a second time over the New England Patriots and Tom Brady. We were that close to getting there. But we felt *great* about Coach Harbaugh and our next season. Everyone had us as an NFC favorite to reach the Super Bowl in 2012, Harbaugh's second season coaching in the pros.

The first big change Coach Harbaugh made that second year was at the quarterback position. We had Colin Kaepernick waiting in the wings because Alex Smith was doing so well as the starter. I mean, we had just gone 13–3 with Alex and were one win away from the Super Bowl. But then, in the middle of the 2012 season, Alex came down with a concussion against the Rams, and Colin Kaepernick came on in the end for a game that ended in a tie. There's no denying that Kaepernick played really well that next week while Alex was still out, and that was it. He would never get his starting position back in San Francisco.

As everyone knows, Colin Kaepernick could run with a long stride, and he had a big, strong arm too. He was more dynamic and explosive at the quarterback position, and Coach Harbaugh liked that he gave us more options on offense as a runner, where we could use more read option pass plays and stuff from college. But Kaepernick also had more zip on his passes and could throw it farther than Alex. We immediately had a quarterback controversy on our hands once Alex was healthy again and ready to reclaim his starting position. Coach Harbaugh wasn't ready to give it to him, and he rode Kaepernick's big arm and legs all the way to Super Bowl XLVII (47), after beating the Atlanta Falcons in a 28–24 comeback in the NFC Championship game.

We were down seventeen points in that game. Atlanta Falcons All-Pro wide receiver Julio Jones was killing us. I think he had over a hundred yards receiving and a touchdown in the *first quarter*. Once we came back on them, it was one of the biggest NFC Championship comebacks in NFL history.

I remember I hit it off with Colin Kaepernick right off the bat because of practice. We had an opportunity to get our timing down and I became very comfortable with his passes. So, we were in sync right away when he started playing. He was also in sync with our top wide receiver, Michael Crabtree, who was able to get downfield for us. We included Randy Moss, who came out of retirement to play for us that year. But he wasn't the Randy Moss we were used to seeing in his prime in Minnesota and then with Tom Brady in New England. Everyone knew that Crabtree was the dude at that point. So, Randy Moss didn't get that many passes.

You know, Crabtree was a great new talent because of his play at the college level. He came out of Texas Tech with a bunch of records in receptions, yards, and touchdowns. Even though Randy Moss had broken all kinds of records at the college and pro level in his career, at his age, and after coming out of retirement, he was no longer that dude on the field like that. But Crabtree was. He had an ability to run great routes, catch the ball in traffic, and make people miss once he got the ball in his hands. He just had a great combination of things that he could do to be effective for us on the football field. He was a cool guy to hang around with too. He just had that all-around cool factor, like a Deion Sanders kind of vibe. People just liked being around him.

We still had Frank Gore too, who had an easier time running the ball once Kaepernick started to run with it because the defenses were forced to pick their poison. The question became:

PLAYING BALL

Are you going to key on Frank Gore running or Colin Kaepernick? So, both of them ended up having big games rushing the ball, until we ended up in the Super Bowl against Jim Harbaugh's older brother, John Harbaugh, and the Baltimore Ravens, who had a tough defense of their own, especially against the run. Their quarterback, Joe Flacco, was having an excellent playoff season that year. So, we had our hands full that game.

Then you had all of the media talk about the Harbaugh brothers going up against each other as Super Bowl coaches. They even started calling it "The Har Bowl" after the two Harbaugh brothers. Once the game started, the Ravens jumped all over us with three touchdown passes from Joe Flacco, while we couldn't get our offense going. We just kept getting penalties and turning the ball over, things that Coach Jim Harbaugh always coached against. When you turn the ball over, you lose ball games. We were down like 28–6 until we had a power outage at the stadium; all of the lights went out in the second half for about thirty minutes. That's when we were able to climb back into the game with a 25–6 swing that got us within one touchdown of winning.

With the score at 34–29, Baltimore, we needed just one more touchdown to take an improbable lead in the game. After a big catch from Crabtree, and a thirty-three-yard run by Frank Gore, we were down on Baltimore's 7-yard line with four downs to score and a little more than two minutes left in the game.

What happened next became sports history. After one running play, we called three straight passes, all to Michael Crabtree in the end zone, and we couldn't complete any of them. So, we ran out of downs inside Baltimore's 5-yard line, and the Ravens took a safety in the end zone to give us two points and punt it away, instead of them possibly turning the ball over near their own end zone. We ended up losing the game, 34–31 as the time ran out on us.

The Super Bowl experience was just a great feeling. After we

came back and won that NFC Championship game against Atlanta, we were *stoked*! We knew we were finally going to the desti-
nation we had been waiting for and fighting for our entire lives,
which was the Super Bowl.

Making it to the Super Bowl is something few and far between. Many football players never get the opportunity to make
it that far. So, we were *psyched*! And so were everybody's families.
We all had to pull together our plans for accommodations for
our families. We started trying to figure out what it was going to
be like and were asking a ton of questions. We had lots of meetings about security and a bunch of other serious issues. You
know, the NFL wanted to inform us on how security was going to
approach things; making sure everyone would be safe was such
a highly detailed job. I mean, the game is that *big*, a super-huge
event.

The Super Bowl has become the biggest event of the year in
any sport. I remember all kinds of media networks started to
come to our facility. We got free commercial products too, from
headphones, to sneakers, to clothes. Promotional companies
were just sending stuff, hoping that we would wear some of it
during our media talks. There was such a great deal of commotion going on that you could get distracted from what we had to
look out for. We had an eleven p.m. curfew to keep us out of
trouble at night. We also had beefed-up security on every hotel
floor.

For my family and friends out of DC and Maryland, I ended
up getting approximately thirty tickets for that Super Bowl. It
was the Super Bowl—a once-in-a-lifetime event—so I did what I
had to do. It was a *mess* getting everyone where they were supposed to be because the game was down in New Orleans that
year, and you had to get there first, find a hotel room, and make
it to the game on time. My grandmother and grandfather both
watched the game from home. I don't think Otis made it down

to New Orleans either. It was just a hell of a night, man. A hell of a night! I just wished we had won it. I've never said anything about not getting any opportunities to score down in that Red Zone. I just stayed in my lane and played the game the way the coaches asked me to.

That next season, the 49ers general manager Trent Baalke—who came in with Harbaugh—decided to trade quarterback Alex Smith to the Kansas City Chiefs, with Coach Andy Reid over there, while Colin Kaepernick was penciled in as our day one starter for the 2013 season. I had another great season of scoring touchdowns that year, with thirteen again, and made the Pro Bowl with nine other 49ers, including Frank Gore and Patrick Willis again.

After going 12–4 with Colin Kaepernick that year and losing the NFC West Division title to the Seattle Seahawks, we lost the NFC Championship game to "The Legion of Doom" Seahawks again in a close 23–17 game. Then the Seahawks went on to embarrass Peyton Manning and the Denver Broncos in Super Bowl XLVIII (48) by a lopsided score of 43–8. Man, we really felt like that should have been *our* Super Bowl title that year. After that third season with Coach Jim Harbaugh, everything started to fall apart.

My momentum got interrupted in 2014 when I started having injury problems again. This time my ankle and back started acting up. As a result, my good times in San Francisco started going downhill. I wasn't playing up to par anymore, and the team didn't do well either. Come to think of it, nobody did well that year. Our record dropped back down to 8–8 and we finished third in our division, behind the Seattle Seahawks and the Arizona Cardinals.

A lot of people call it "the Super Bowl hangover," especially when you lose. Once you make it to a Super Bowl, you often have all these players you have to square away with new contracts. Then you'll have players who want to leave the team for better deals with other teams, so you end up bringing in new guys to fill those holes.

I believe with us, it was a combination of all those different things. You'll have players who are no longer happy because they're not getting their contract needs met, and that can really become a team breaker. You also have to keep in mind that when you go to a Super Bowl, sometimes players can start feeling themselves, where different guys start to think they're the best in the game and want top dollar for it, even when they still have obvious things to work on. That's when the morale of the team starts changing, and players start losing their humility.

The next thing we knew, Jim Harbaugh and Trent Baalke started going at it behind closed doors. I think it was, like, a control issue, where Jim Harbaugh wanted a different level of control over the players we drafted, traded for, and everything else. So, they got to the point where they had bad blood, and Harbaugh didn't like the short end of the stick he was getting, so he ended up leaving after that final season.

None of us really knew the specifics of what went on between them, but we were kind of appalled by it. After Coach Harbaugh came in and showed us how to win like that, we wanted to keep it going and playing for him. So, we just couldn't figure out why they would let him walk away like that. I mean, how is it that we're winning all these games and the coach just up and leaves us like that? We didn't know what was going on and it didn't make any sense to us. Coach Harbaugh never said anything about their dispute out in public. Then he ended up taking a college job at the University of Michigan instead of another NFL job, so that let us know it was about him having more control.

Then the team promoted Jim Tomsula to head coach. He was coaching our defensive line. That didn't make sense to us either. Everyone assumed the offensive coordinator, Greg Roman, would get the job. Then they started letting teammates go, starting with my good friend, running back Frank Gore, who ended up signing a free-agent deal with the Indianapolis Colts. He had been the most consistent guy on offense, just like Patrick Willis had been our most consistent guy on defense. When Frank Gore left, and then Patrick Willis retired that year because of issues with his feet, that kind of signaled the beginning of the end for us, and we knew that the team was looking to rebuild and start all over again. Coach Harbaugh had been San Francisco's best coach for *years*, right up until they signed Coach Kyle Shanahan to lead the team. Before that, everything started going downhill. A lot of guys weren't playing the same. I wasn't playing up to par, and the team just wasn't working things out.

I don't remember Colin Kaepernick being that talkative about politics and race issues when he was first on the team, so it just came out of nowhere for everybody when he started kneeling before the games during the national anthem. When he first got there, he fit right in. "Kap" was really cool with everybody. He was a great human being. But I guess he changed with the girlfriend he started dating. That's what everyone was talking about, but we weren't sure. Personally, I didn't know what it was about. I was just trying to figure it out. Then the whole Kaepernick disposition, with him kneeling before the games to protest racism became this big national issue for all of the teams and players that year. I didn't expect him to do that.

Up until then, I had never seen Kaepernick do anything like that. He never protested anything that I saw. I wasn't with the team anymore by the time it all happened, so when I saw it, I thought to myself, *Wow, this is different. I see what he's trying to do.* However, I didn't think he was going to keep going with it. I thought he would make a little U-turn once the pressure started for him to stop kneeling, but he didn't. Nobody even saw him going in that direction. I know *I* didn't. But I saw what he was trying to do. I can't knock that. Whether we agreed with his approach or not, he had a good cause because racism does still exist in America.

However, there was a lot of turmoil swirling around Kaepernick and teammate Aldon Smith, who played defensive end; he and Colin didn't see eye to eye over a woman Aldon was dating who Kap started dating. The conversation was that she kind of just hopped over onto Colin's side. So, there was a lot of turmoil in the locker room over that because Aldon was highly upset about it. They even had a physical fight, supposedly. The next thing you know, Aldon Smith was being released from the team for having several arrests for DUIs (Driving Under the Influence of alcohol) and other team discipline issues.

Well, Smith was one of the best players on the team at that point, and he was still in the early years of his career. That just goes to show you how quickly things can fall apart. San Francisco wasn't winning anymore. There was just too much division going on that started as soon as we knew that Coach Jim Harbaugh was on his way out. That's when things just went crazy, and they went haywire really quick. All kinds of destructive stuff started going on in the locker room.

Fortunately, the down year in 2014 didn't hurt my business investment deal with Fantex because if you think about it, you can't control the market in any business. Sometimes you might take a hit. Sometimes you're up, sometimes you're down. However, it wasn't just about me. I wasn't the only guy on the platform that the company was going after. There were a lot of different ball players they were considering; I just happened to be one of the first to do it. In fact, I was the first *athlete* to do it. But it seemed like it was mostly football players. Even though I started getting injured again, my stock was already established. So, you ride the wave up and down like you would with any other stock.

Reflecting back on it all, I think my value pretty much stayed the same because, after a while, the company planned to go from private to public stock, which usually increased the value a lot when more people can buy into it. They also had plans to change the name when the company went public. When they finally took the company public, with the way my stock underperformed, I don't think the company followed through on all of the plans they had to market. I don't know the reason, but maybe their business model wasn't doing as well as they expected it to.

That was also around the time that my youngest brother, Michael, started getting into trouble in DC, and one day my family called me up to tell me that he had killed a man by hitting him upside the head with a hammer. It was my grandmother who called and told me about it when it happened. I was so caught off guard by it because I never really thought anything like that would happen. I didn't have any conversations with my brother about what he was doing and what he was getting into. All along, it was hard for me to have a conversation with him because he didn't want to talk. By the time my grandmother told me what happened, Michael had already been arrested. Like I said earlier, some people thought he had been set up because he was already having some mental problems. It's not so unreasonable to think that other people could have taken advantage of his mental instability.

When I hit that next season of 2015 with San Francisco, I think it was the last year of my contract, so negotiations for the next deal were coming around. We never got a chance to talk about it, though. Before everything went down on my deal to the Denver Broncos, I never heard about any trade talks. I never heard anything. It just kind of hit me out of the blue.

First of all, it seemed Jim Harbaugh had already agreed with the team owners to step away after the 2014 season, when we missed the playoffs with another 8–8 record. And, as I said, the team then elevated the defensive line coach, Jim Tomsula, to the head coaching job. So, changes were already being made with the team before they spoke to me about my future there.

I remember we won the first game against the Minnesota Vikings that year, and then lost four games straight after that. I was still leading the team in receptions and yards. However, we just weren't scoring any points, so guys were already talking about the team tanking to get better draft picks.

I received a text from Trent Baalke, the 49ers general manager, telling me to head into his office when I arrived at practice. This was the day after we lost to the St. Louis Rams in another blowout game. I was home resting up and I could tell by the urgency of Trent's message that something was up. I could sense it.

He didn't tip his hand or say anything major in the text. It simply said, **"Come see me when you get here."** He didn't say anything else. I kind of sensed that something was wrong. So, I walked into Trent Baalke's office at the 49ers' facility and asked him, "What's up?" I had no idea what he wanted to talk to me about. I just stood there and waited.

Trent said, "Take a seat, Vernon."

I sat down.

Then he said, "We're thinking about trading you."

I took a deep breath and let it out. By that time, I had put in a lot of dues in San Fransico, and in the league, and I had a contract that would continue with the next team. I wasn't that worried about it anymore, or least not as I was when I sat down with Coach Singletary.

I nodded to Trent and said, "Okay. I figured something was up."

I'd had a good eight-year run with the team, and I realized that nothing lasts forever. It was about time for a change. After that, Trent Baalke pulled up three different teams. I think one was Miami, the second team I can't remember, and the third was Denver.

He said, "I think the Broncos would be the best fit for you because they got a great chance of going back to the Super Bowl. I think it would be an amazing opportunity for you."

At the time, the Broncos were still undefeated that season, while we had, like, five or six losses already. So, it wasn't a bad deal at all for me to head off to Denver under those circumstances. Trent presented me with the three teams because he respected me and wanted to be fair to me.

Initially, my thoughts and emotions hit me like a flash. But once I thought about it, I just couldn't *believe* what Trent was telling me. My time in San Francisco was up, and I was going crazy wondering, *Why?* I was still one of the top offensive weapons on the team. I didn't know what to do or say to him. Many things were going through my head at that moment. I wanted to call Janel and tell her about it, so she could get ready for a move with our kids. Then I thought about calling my grandmother to let her know. But I opted to tell Janel first.

Our conversation about it was very short. I called her up and said, "This is what's going on right now. The general manager said there may be a chance of San Francisco trading me. But you won't have to be in San Francisco all that time." I paused, took a deep breath, and told her, "This all kind of caught me by surprise."

Janel said, "It'll be okay, Vernon. It'll be okay." She was always supportive like that. We had been through many different hard decisions and issues while trying to raise a family on the road. Then she started asking me how I felt about the trade.

"It's bittersweet, to be honest. It's bittersweet because the team feels like we're tanking now, and I think I'm ready to move on to a different situation," I admitted to her.

That's what I told Janel, and it was true. The team was rebuilding, and I was ready to move on. Although everything worked out in my favor, it was still tough for me to leave after playing for the 49ers for my first ten years in the pros. They had drafted me and developed me as a Pro Bowl–caliber player, and

163

when you stay somewhere for ten years, you're like, *Wow, this is really going to be an adjustment.*

Janel was always on my side, so I told her I was going to go do what I had to do and go on from there. I just didn't expect the 49ers to get rid of me right then and there. I liked San Francisco. Once we lost that Super Bowl to Baltimore and didn't get our mojo back, it seemed like the 49ers were looking to rebuild again, while Denver was a Super Bowl–bound team already, and they had Peyton Manning as their quarterback. It was pretty much a no-brainer for me. I would get a chance to catch passes from a future Hall of Famer. I just had to deal with the reality that I would no longer be a San Francisco 49er. That was the bitter part of the deal.

I was definitely excited about catching passes from Peyton Manning, and my family was too, or at least the ones who knew football. That part of the trade was sweet. There was also a part of me that *wanted* to leave along with a part that didn't. You know, my emotions continued to be a tug-of-war. When an organization is looking to start over, it's never good for veteran players, and that's what I was at that point. So, if they were getting rid of me and many of our other veteran guys were leaving, what else were they trying to do but rebuild? I had to look at the Denver Broncos trade as a fresh start. I really appreciated the fact that Trent had given me an option of where to go. He gave me a hug after our trade meeting, and I hugged him back. Then I went and cleaned out my locker, while calling everyone I needed to talk to.

I walked away from the 49ers facility with tears in my eyes. I was definitely hurt, but at the same time, I understood it. The NFL was a *business,* and the time had come for me to move on to the next chapter of my life and career. Trying to hide my bittersweet emotions, I walked around the locker room, shaking everyone's hand and giving daps to whoever was there that day.

Then I went and said goodbye to the owner. I literally walked through the entire building saying my goodbyes. Then I got in my car and drove home. The whole time, I thought about how to deal with Janel and our kids, while figuring everything out.

During those last two years of my career in San Francisco, Janel and my children were living with me full time. Janel wanted to keep that closeness going, where the kids could always see me. She figured they had gotten used to it. I ended up leaving the Bay Area for Denver the next day, and Janel and the kids came out a week after me. I got settled and found a place in Denver. However, I didn't advise Janel to put our kids in school at their Mile High Academy. I told her I was coming right back to the Bay Area and to DC after the season, whether we went to the Super Bowl with Denver or not.

I had business relationships and all kinds of things going on in the Bay Area, and DC would always be home during the off-season. But Janel had already decided to take the kids out of school in the Bay Area and enroll them in a school in Denver. After the season was over, just like I already knew, Janel came right back to San Jose. I figured it would have been best if she just stayed there with the kids in the first place. She could have flown in to visit me in Denver anytime if she wanted to. The flight to Denver from San Francisco was only two and a half hours.

I got out to Denver, and they had things rolling just like we did when we went to the Super Bowl in San Francsico that year. You could just feel it in the winning culture. After Denver had lost the previous Super Bowl to Seattle a few years before, they basically kept their team together and added pieces to it for another run. That's why they were bringing me in. It was an all-hands-on-deck mentality to bring in more guys who they thought could help them to win. I think they were still undefeated that season when I first got there. I mean, they were playing some good football.

They had Head Coach Gary Kubiak leading the team that

year, with a championship defense and a championship offense. There were a lot of similarities over there to what we had in San Franscico during our championship run. Everyone seemed to be positive in the locker room. The players were all upbeat. Everyone came to practice ready to go. It was obvious that practice was very important to the team.

You know, they were healthy and practiced at a fast pace because when teams have guys who are all banged up, the production at practice slows down. Coaches then start to pull back a little bit. Then you don't really get the production you need in the games because you're not getting it from practice. So, the Denver similarities to our San Franscico team were common.

The Broncos roster was loaded too that year. We had Peyton Manning at quarterback, Emmanuel Sanders and Demaryius Thomas at receivers. Our running backs were C. J. Anderson and Ronnie Hillman. Von Miller and DaMarcus Ware were getting after the quarterback on defense. We had Brandon Marshall and Danny Trevathan as linebackers. Aqib Talib and Chris Harris as our lockdown cornerbacks. I mean, the team was loaded. They were built for a championship run, and then they brought me in there.

I remember I became really good friends with DeMarcus Ware, who had come over from Dallas. He was one of the guys I really connected with in Denver. He was a really good dude.

Of course we eventually lost a game or two that year in Denver. No team is going undefeated. That's very hard to do in any professional sport. Of course we knew we would lose at some point, as long as it wasn't in the Super Bowl, like New England did that one year when they went 18–0, only to lose to the New York Giants in the Super Bowl.

Cam Newton and the Carolina Panthers had a spectacular season themselves that year. Cam Newton was named the MVP (Most Valuable Player) of the whole NFL, and I think they were 15–1 during the regular season. Cam was really playing at a high level, and we knew that we had to deal with him to win. He was basically the key to the game. At the time, he was one of the best quarterbacks in the league. Cam was better than Peyton Manning at that point. He was playing with energy and enthusiasm, and he was just hitting on all cylinders. The game plan we had for him worked beautifully. The defense got after Cam every time he dropped back and had him running around like crazy on every play. We sacked him seven times that game and forced four turnovers, including a big Cam Newton fumble in the end zone.

Man, we jumped all over Carolina and kept the pressure on Cam Newton all game long for a hard-earned 24–10 Super Bowl victory. Ironically, after being traded to Denver, we ended up playing that Super Bowl 50 at the 49ers Levi's Stadium, back in Santa Clara, California. So, I got traded to Denver and ended up winning the Super Bowl right back at Levi's. We were even in the San Franscisco side of the locker room instead of the visiting side.

I kept the Super Bowl tickets light for that one. I had a few people come out, but most of my family and friends just watched it at home, including my grandmother Adaline and grandfather Lynwood again. A whole bunch of my guys called to congratulate me after the win, though. I had a lot of old teammates calling me. It was just an unbelievable feeling to finally win it!

After that half season and Super Bowl win in Denver, I immediately became a free agent, waiting for new teams to contact me about playing. But reports were saying that a lot of teams figured I was washed up by then. I don't know how they could have believed that because I had just had a great year out in Denver. I didn't catch as many passes as normal, but my blocking had become a new strength.

I remember Peyton called me as soon as I got out to Denver. He started the conversation by asking me, "When did you get in?" We mainly just talked to get familiar with each other. But we never really had time to work out with routes or anything because we were already in midseason when I joined the team. I remember Peyton had, like, twenty ice bags all over his body when I walked into the facility to see him the first time. So, he wasn't throwing any extra footballs or anything of that nature with me. He just wanted to talk to me, which was fine.

I only played with Peyton for that half of a season. And his playbook was *extensive*. I'm not even going to lie! If I had known I had to learn so much in so little time, I wouldn't have gone to Denver, because it was a great deal of stress on me, especially at midseason, trying to learn the big playbook that Peyton Manning had.

Normally, it takes from April to summer camp in July to study a new playbook if you're headed to another team. Teams usually pick you up in March or April after the previous season. Then you have that time, from April all the way up until September, to learn your new playbook, and that's plenty of time to do it. But even then, Peyton's playbook would have been extra to learn. That's probably why I didn't get more receptions in Denver's offense. I wasn't that familiar with what they were doing.

I did a great job with my blocking in Denver, though. That's what they asked me to do. If they asked me to run a route, I could do that too. I could clearly still play ball. The only problem was not knowing Peyton's plays. So, when I became a free agent, I assumed that teams were taking a slow approach of reaching out to me. You know, they were taking their time with it. Maybe they thought I was going to be too expensive, and teams didn't think I would be worth it. Then my hometown team of Washington reached out to me.

Their general manager, Scott McCloughan, brought me in for a visit and talks with the team. Ironically, he was in a general manager position with San Francisco when they first drafted me in 2006, so we were already familiar with each other, and Scott knew what I was capable of. So, I took the visit back home to

Washington, and they were pretty much the only team that was really interested in me. Maybe if I had waited, some other teams would have popped up on the radar, but it was all good to be back home. I could spend more quality time with my family and old friends, and they could see me play again at home.

I knew I was going to have to prove myself again. I would have to do that wherever I went. Washington was still home, though, with my family and friends, so I went ahead and signed with Washington, taking a pay cut because they were still excited about my talent and willing to sign me for the long haul if the first year worked out. You could basically call my first year with Washington a prove-it deal, which meant they signed me to a one-year contract to see if I could still play at a high level.

I said, "Cool," and sat down to sign the one-year deal because I knew I could still play. As they say, I was willing to bet on myself to get a new, long-term deal instead of another short one.

After signing with them, I walked around the building and sat with Head Coach Jay Gruden. He told me, "Jordan Reed and Niles Paul are the two guys in the building who you'll need to compete with at tight end."

I nodded and replied, "Cool. I don't have a problem with that." I was always about competition.

On my first day of practice, everyone was going crazy because they had never seen me go all-out on team drills like I always did. They had no coach on the staff or players on the team who had ever seen me run or work out. I was still fast, particularly as a big guy. I've always been able to move for my size, running faster than most of the guys they had on the team.

My practices in Washington became their first opportunity to see me work, and they were all impressed to witness me running the way I did. I mean, I was still flying around, man! I just learned to do everything with urgency. The Broncos team was just as shocked when I practiced with them out in Denver. They were all looking at me flying around too. I've always practiced hard like that. I ran full speed, full throttle anytime I lined up on the field. That left the players and the coaches in awe.

By the time the regular season started for Washington, I was playing so well that Scott called my agent in midseason and wanted to sign me for three more years. So, we went and signed the deal for three more years and got my stock value back up as a still valuable player. The new deal came in at three years for $15 million. Of course it wasn't on par with the five-year and $37 million deal in San Francisco, but $15 million was still good money after playing ten years in the league. In order to sign that three-year deal, I had to play for one year and $1 million in a show-and-prove agreement to let them all see that I could still play. And like I said, I most definitely could.

Chapter 10
Back at Home

WHEN I WENT BACK HOME AND PLAYED FOR WASHINGTON from 2016 to 2019, Kirk Cousins was the quarterback for the first two years, and then he left and signed with Minnesota. After him we had Alex Smith, who I started my career with in San Francisco. It's interesting how I got to start my career and then nearly finish it with Alex Smith. He even won the Comeback Player of the Year award in our last year together in 2019. Alex Smith had gone through some gruesome injuries in his professional football career, particularly to his legs. So, he ended up retiring the same year that I did.

Of course, once I returned home to the DC and Maryland area, I had my mother to deal with again. While I was in San Francisco, I was so far away, I didn't have to deal with her too much. I pretty much was able to keep my distance from her, which was what I wanted. I still spoke with her, I just wasn't around to see her. Our physical distance and separation kept a lot of her sticky situations away from me. We mostly just talked over the phone.

Our conversations were really basic. I'd call her up and say,

"Hey, Ma, I'm just checking in on you. How are you doing? I'm just checking to make sure you're in good spirits."

That was pretty much the extent of it. I would never talk to her about anything too deep. If I started talking to her for too long, she'd start asking me for money. She pulled that stunt on me all the time.

"Let me hold a couple of dollars so I can get my hair done. I need a couple of dollars to get some food," was how she'd ask me for it.

When she first started doing that, and I had the extra money, I would give her two hundred dollars or so at a time. Usually, she would be okay with that. But I had to be careful too, because my mother was still spending money on drugs and then lie to us about it. Whenever she said she needed money for something specific, I would give it to my grandmother to manage it. She would make sure that my mother used the money for the necessary things and not spend it on drugs. So, my grandmother, Adaline, would get what my mother needed.

Believe me, it was hard telling my mother "No" all the time. Sometimes, I would give her fifty or a hundred dollars to see what she did with it. But it was still the same act with her; you didn't know if she really used the money for what she said she needed it for, or if she used it to buy drugs again.

When I came back to the DMV area to play for Washington, I reached out to my mother in earnest to cultivate a new relationship between us. I was pleasantly surprised when I saw her again during my first couple of times back because she looked like she was doing much better. In fact, she looked *really* good. She looked like she had her stuff together, and that gave me hope. It appeared as though she was trying hard to change her ways. Not wanting to rock the boat, I never asked her specific questions anymore. I just wanted her to know that I cared about her.

One day I asked her, "Hey, Ma, how are you? You want to go out to dinner? You want to go with me and the kids to Miami?

It'll be great to have somebody in Miami with us. So, if I want to step out or whatever, you can keep an eye on the kids for me."

By then, Janel and I had gone our separate ways. As I said, without us ever getting married, we eventually grew apart. So, I was taking the kids to Miami by myself that year, to participate in the *Baywatch* movie premiere as a cast member of the film.

"Yeah, I'll go to Miami," my mother responded with excitement. That was good to hear and music to my ears.

I ended up taking my mother to Miami to attend the movie premiere of *Baywatch*, starring Dwayne Johnson, The Rock. I was only in one small scene, but I was still in it and had been invited to the premiere. That was back in 2017, and it was the first time I had taken my mother somewhere with me. Actually, it was the first time I ever left my mother with my kids without me or Janel to supervise her. Before then, I never felt confident about allowing her to babysit my kids; I had this fear that she'd just get up and leave them alone by themselves, like she did with me and my siblings, and I didn't want that to happen to my kids. There was no way I wanted them to feel the abandonment I had.

Well, my mother went along with us to Miami for the *Baywatch* premiere, and we ended up having a nice family dinner on South Beach. From there we went on a couple of other trips, like out to Virginia Beach. Then we started going on smaller, local excursions, like to the zoo. We went to amusement parks and many things that made us draw closer to one another. All of the activities I did with my mother in that short period of time in DC were special. I ended up doing more things with her in those Washington years than I'd ever done with her in my entire life. Taking her places with me was the ideal way of cultivating a great relationship with her. I always wanted to do that with my mother, I just had to get around to doing it.

As you now know, many of the experiences I had with my mother in the past hadn't been that great. So, I wanted to spend a lot more time with her. And I did. I did as much as I could with her when I got back home to DC. By then, I had grown up and become a mature man who could learn how to navigate a healthy and meaningful relationship with his mother.

With more wisdom accumulated, I was getting better at understanding things. Like I said, I always wanted to get closer to my mother. It had been on my mind for *years*, especially after returning home to play for Washington. I just had that nagging feeling that there was a lot more I could do to help my mother. So, it became a new goal of mine.

I was pretty adamant about helping my mother out. At that stage in my life, it was imperative that I connect with her in ways that I had never imagined. She even started coming out to my house in Leesburg, Virginia. I must admit that I remained nervous about leaving her around the kids for too long, though. That was just the nature of learning to trust her again. We could never really tell if she was clean or back on drugs. There was always suspicion of her, but you couldn't tell for sure.

However, there were two things I was totally sure of that my mother continued to do: She started smoking more marijuana and she was still drinking a lot. Whenever she drank, you had to watch what you said around her because she would snap on you so fast. She would always get extra-aggressive when she drank. Mostly, she would be verbally aggressive with people. Sometimes, if you rubbed her the wrong way, she could get physically aggressive too. For example, if you offended her in any way while she was drinking, she'd be ready to go off on you, like a ticking time bomb.

In the meantime, she would always brag about how tough she was. "This is tough! I'm tough! I'm a soldier!" she stated.

When my mother wasn't drinking or high on drugs, she was the sweetest person you could ever meet in your life. But once she got to drinking her beers, it was like she would turn into an entirely different person. It was like night and day. When we were growing up, my mother would drink Colt 45 and Miller beers. She also drank Heineken. And she loved to smoke cigarettes too: Newport 100s. Because of all the trauma that I went through as a kid, I never smoked or drank. It just wasn't for me.

When I came back home and played for Washington, I gave my mother tickets to the games. In fact, since my family was still living in DC, Maryland, and Virginia, we had a whole section for the games. My mother typically got along well with the other parents and family members at the games. They were all rooting for us on the same team.

My mother got along really well with Janel too. But I was in charge of whether or not she got to be around our kids because they didn't have that kind of relationship with her. It was more cordiality and respect for your elders whenever they saw my mother. Outside of that, Janel and the kids didn't have a firm relationship with my mother. Neither one of us was around her enough to have a deeper relationship.

Janel had relationships with everyone else, though. She brought the children around my grandmother Adaline and my grandfather Lynwood all the time. She knew all of my brothers and sisters. She even had a relationship with Otis. Janel was probably closest to my sister Christina because she would come to visit us regularly, even when we were out in California. Christina flew out to San Francisco to see us a lot. Over time, the kids grew to love their Aunt Christina. They were just really familiar with her.

My aunts, Patty and Sharon, came out to California to visit us a few times too. My mother only came out that one time to the game that she got into an argument about. That was either 2013 or 2014, when Vontae was playing for the Indianapolis Colts, and they played us in San Francisco. My mother came because that was the first time Vontae and I would play against each other. However, she didn't even end up coming to the game.

Aunt Patty and my sister Christina had also flown out to California to see the game between me and Vontae. Instead of going to the game as planned, what happened was the night before the game, I invited a lot of people over to my house. As she had a habit of doing, my mother got to drinking and started using profanity around the children, and Janel got mad at her. The next thing you know, Janel had said something abrasive to my mother. In return, my mother said something back to her. The situation escalated really fast.

In an attempt to defuse the situation, I tried to calm my mother down. "Ma, you got to watch what you say around the kids. And you gotta respect Janel in her house. This is *our house*, and you gotta respect that," I said to her.

Then my mother started going crazy, as if I didn't have the right to tell her that. You know, she got all rebellious. She started saying stuff like, "I don't have to do *nothing*. I don't even have to go to this damn *game* if I don't want to. You don't tell me what to do."

She was just mouthing off and acting crazy. So, I put her out of the house and had to get an escort to take her back to her hotel room. I had friends and family members who were staying over at the house that night, while others stayed at the hotel. We even had one of my mother's best friends out there with her, my godmother, Patty Duke. But she couldn't calm my mother down either. She ended up going back to the hotel room with her.

I mean, my mother had a full-blown episode right in front of my friends, family, and teammates. I even broke down and started crying over it. I remember saying, "Man, my mom can never do *anything*! She always makes stuff *hard*, yelling and raising her voice like she's back in the neighborhood in DC."

I lived in a great neighborhood out in California that was nothing like what we had coming up in DC. Yet my mother became loud and obnoxious, as if she was still walking around out on Georgia Avenue. It got to the point where she was nearly ready to fight Janel in the house. And I was so over it, man. It was *embarrassing*.

I shook my head and said, "No, I can't do this." I had to let my mother know that she was wrong. After all of the chaos, she ended up not even coming to the game. I think she just stayed back at the hotel. I don't even think she watched the game on TV. I don't know what she did. I didn't see my mother again for about a *year* after that. But I did go to see her before she left California. I felt like I had to. The rest of the family had come out to the game that day, but not my mother. I think it may have been eight people in total.

Obviously, my mother had really rubbed Janel that bad, while trying to fight her inside the house like that. For me, it was more disappointment because I loved Janel. She was the mother of my children. I also had love for my mother, so it was really embarrassing and hurtful for them to get into an argument like that before the game.

I would never want to disrespect my mother, but she disrespected Janel in our house. That made things really awkward. The whole family was upset by it. My mother had acted out right in front of everyone. Eventually, Janel smoothed everything out. But that's how things went down when my mother came out to California with us.

When I relocated back to the DMV, I already had the house out in Leesburg. I also had to buy Janel and the kids a house in Maryland when we broke up because she would've had them back in DC if I hadn't. I didn't want the kids growing up or living in DC. Once we broke up, I tried to tell myself that whatever Janel did with her personal life had nothing to do with me. I just had to do what I could to fulfill my duties and obligations of providing for my children and their mother. And I did just that. If Janel had gone out and gotten married to someone else, that would have been different. She would've stopped being my responsibility. We would've had to figure it all out.

Once I got back to the DMV area, I spent a lot of time by myself and with the kids. I would get them every holiday, weekend, or whenever I was off during football season. If they had to go to school, or if I had to head back to work, we would change things up accordingly. Friday night was usually my time with the kids, and then on Saturday morning they would head back home. Then I would get them on Christmas, Thanksgiving, and other major holidays. Sometimes I had to hire a nanny to help me out with the kids because I was so busy with football. Eventually, my kids wound up loving sports too.

When Jianni was younger, he started playing flag football, and right away, I could tell that he would be good. Just like me, he was bigger than the average kid. In fact, all of my kids are bigger than average. At sixteen, Jianni is already six-two and 220 pounds. That's a big boy! He now plays defensive end at DeMatha Catholic High School. He's doing really well with it, at one of the top football schools in Maryland. He used to play basketball too, but he stopped to focus on football.

My younger son, Valaughn, plays soccer. He wanted to play football too, but I wanted him to wait until he got older. He's already massive at just nine years old. I also think my kids should run track because I know they all can run. My kids are big, fast, and skillful, from the oldest to the youngest. Valaughn can do some unbelievable things already. He can already catch a football with one hand or over his shoulder, which is pretty impressive at his age.

As for my daughter, Valleigh, she's tough. I don't know what she's going to do yet. We have to figure that out. Right now, she likes singing, dancing, and music. So, she's the artist in the family. I guess she inherited my passion for the arts.

After Janel and I broke up, I met another woman, Kayla, in around 2016, who worked in security for the government. She couldn't tell me exactly what she did. That was confidential. Who knows, she may have been an undercover agent, and revealing too much could have been against their policy. Kayla ended up becoming my fiancée. Ultimately, I didn't marry her

because we couldn't work through the ups and downs of our relationship. It seemed like we weren't on the same page. I felt
that it wasn't really meant for us to get married, and we eventually parted ways.

When I first met Kayla at an all-white gala party in DC, I
thought I was ready to get married. It was a rooftop venue, with
a lot of people in attendance, including a bunch of my teammates. It was my first time out in DC since I had been back home
as a member of the Washington team. The event was organized
by wide receiver Pierre Garçon, who was raising money for char-
ity. He had partnered up with some local people who were raising money for the Boys & Girls Clubs. But it may have been
canceled. I can't quite remember what happened.

The marriage bug ended up being a false alarm. After Kayla
and I got engaged, we started having differences and things just
didn't go as we expected them to. We had some issues that we
needed to work out. However, no matter how hard we tried, we
couldn't get past our issues.

Through that experience, I learned that a working relationship always takes two willing participants. But I didn't think we
were equally yoked. So, it was my decision not to go forward
with the marriage. Kayla felt differently about it, however. She
said, "I don't think this is a situation where we need to stop moving forward with the wedding. We just need to get therapy. We
need to work this out."

I didn't feel that way about it at all. I didn't feel comfortable
with the marriage idea anymore, so I didn't want to go through
with it. I didn't care about getting therapy. I knew what I knew,
and I didn't feel comfortable with moving forward. I don't even
think I consulted with Pastor Erwin on that one. I just *knew*.

Then I reconnected with a couple of folks I knew from my
high school and neighborhood days in DC. I got involved with a
lot of different functions and events during the season or just
from being around the District again. When you get older, you

realize that the city is very small. You end up seeing a lot of the people you grew up with and people you used to be around. That happened at the clubs, after the games, or just from hanging out around DC.

The team wasn't doing too well when I played for Washington. We almost made the playoffs in 2016 with an 8–7–1 record with Kirk Cousins, with a game that ended in a tie against Cincinnati. However, after that first year, we just couldn't get over the hump. We were just never good enough to make the playoffs with Kirk Cousins. Then he left for a big-money contract to play in Minnesota, and we got Alex Smith, who ended up with a bad leg injury after the first year, which opened the door for Case Keenum and Dwayne Haskins to step up.

However, none of our quarterbacks played well enough to make the playoffs. They did just enough to be average. I had a few flashy plays here and there in Washington, and a couple of touchdowns each year to show that I could still play. But we didn't do anything spectacular as a team. Then I suffered a concussion against the New York Giants in September of my final contract year, 2019, and I ended up missing a lot of the season.

The team eventually put me on the injured reserve list. I think I only played four games that last season. I had played fourteen years in the NFL by then, and had been to two Super Bowls, where I lost one and won another. I had already made it to fourteen seasons; I was thinking that I could play six more years and make it to twenty. The team even asked me what I wanted to do, and if I wanted to keep playing.

Honestly, though, the concussion I had that year was a bad one. I was evaluated by the doctors, while the team continued to ask me what I wanted to do. I honestly thought about going forward and continuing with my career. I felt as though I could reach my goal of making it to twenty years in the NFL. That all changed drastically, though after my grandfather, Lynwood, died. That just did a real psychological number on me. His loss made me feel like I couldn't go on anymore.

I remember I was in my bedroom while getting ready to meet up with the team after we had finished our walk-throughs for the game at practice. I had driven home so I could change clothes and get fresh and clean for the trip to Philadelphia to play against the Eagles. That was the beginning of September, right as the season was starting in my final contract year. As I was going out the door, my grandmother called me, and she was crying hysterically.

"He's gone! He's gone!" she cried.

I said, "What? Who's gone?"

"Lynwood. He's left us. He passed this morning."

Right when she said that, I heard sirens in the background. So, I broke down and cried with her. Then I had to pull myself together so I could drive over to my grandparents' house to see what was going on. I jumped in my car, drove back over to my grandmother's, and walked into the house. My grandfather was lying in the back room, dead, with his mouth wide open. We had to call the funeral home instead of the hospital so they could take him to the morgue to prepare his body for the funeral because he was already dead. My uncle helped me carry his body to the vehicle we were going to use to transport him.

I hung around the family for a few more hours after that, but I still had a game to play and a flight to make up to Philadelphia. In my mind, I was still contemplating whether I wanted to go to the game to play. I ended up not traveling with the team that day. However, later on that night, the team owner, Dan Snyder, had his private jet warmed up to fly me up to Philadelphia to help my team try to win a football game, which was nice of him to do.

After my having only two hours of sleep that night, we ended up losing the game, and I called my grandmother early in the morning the next day to check in with her. I just wanted to talk to her to keep her head up and let her know everything was going to be all right. My family was all that I could think of after that game in Philly. I didn't even know how I got through that game up there, to be honest with you. It was all *crazy*! But that's how the 2019 season started out for me.

Even though we lost the game, I had the most miraculous play of my career, where I jumped over two guys and broke several tackles on a long touchdown reception. It felt like my grandfather had lifted me up and catapulted me into the end zone for that play. Ironically, it became the final touchdown of my career.

Over the course of that last year, I started thinking about my life after football and all of the things I wanted to do, like music, movies, art, and so on. I was just trying to figure it all out. I kept thinking to myself, *Man, I really don't know what I want to do. I don't know how it's all going to come together, but I have faith that it's all going to work out.*

I became motivated to start looking at other opportunities I might have, like my small role in the Dwayne Johnson *Baywatch* movie. However, that wasn't the first movie I was in. Prior to *Baywatch* with The Rock, I did an independent Christian movie called *I'm in Love with a Church Girl*, starring rapper Ja Rule, around 2011. I was still with the 49ers at that time, and it was my first small film role. I think the story was even based in the city of San Jose. So, it was a local shoot when I was already there.

Initially, the producer just wanted to use my house to shoot a few scenes. He knew my assistant, Sasha, so they got in touch with me and asked me about it. I said, "Okay, I'll let you use my house." It was no big deal to me. They gave me some money and a small role. If you watch the movie, the house they used was my California home at the time. I play a bouncer in a nightclub, with one line. "I don't want to see you around here again," was all I had to say, while looking mean. Then I had to throw Ja Rule's lead character out of the club, wearing all black with a mohawk haircut. They plugged Jerry Rice into a role in the movie too. But he just played himself. They had a scene where he pops up in a cameo. Someone says, "Hey, that's Jerry Rice." Then they approached him to get his autograph.

When the *Baywatch* movie opportunity came up, a buddy named Dave Weiss linked me up with the production team. I actually met him through the actor Jeremy Renner, who's popular in many films. Jeremy introduced me to Dave after taking me to his cool restaurant on Sunset Boulevard in LA. After that, I became really good friends with Dave too.

Dave started to look out for film roles for me, and he called me up one day and said, "Hey, bro, what are you doing?" It was one of those last-minute calls from him.

I said to him, "I don't have nothing going on right now. I don't have too much on my schedule. Why?"

He said, "I'm down here in Savannah, Georgia, shooting a movie with The Rock called *Baywatch*. We got a part for you. Can you get on a plane and come down to Savannah?"

I wasted no time with my response. I said, "Oh my! Sure. Yeah, let's do that. Get me a plane ticket, and I'll be there first thing!"

Dave said, "Okay, send me your birth date and where you're traveling from. And give me your seat preferences too."

The next thing you know, I was on a plane to Savannah, Georgia. They gave me a role where I was playing basketball. I was just a stranger on the basketball court, with my height and size. In the scene, a guy gets his shot blocked. When the ball gets swatted away, I make the comment, "Man, he was like, Bird," while The Rock's lead character jogs by us on the courts.

I thought it was a cool short scene. The movie was dope, and I liked filming it. It was a short-lived scene, but it was still a great opportunity for me to get my chops wet in a movie. The process is the process, and I was just getting familiar with it. After appearing in those first movies, of course I thought about being in more of them. Then I went ahead and took an acting class to prepare myself for the next role in a movie. I was just trying to figure out how to do it better.

I took a class at the Shelton Theatre of Art in downtown San Francisco. That was either in 2012 or 2013. I would go a couple of days a week to learn the craft. I did that during our offseason. In all, I studied acting for eight weeks. Once you have the training, you never stop doing it. It's like riding a bike; the more you do it and challenge yourself, the better you get at it. Acting was fun too. It was a nice diversion for me. I would go to workouts and practice and, after that, nobody knew what I was doing or what I was up to. I would make a forty-five-minute drive to San Francisco, excited about my acting classes. I was putting in the groundwork just like I did for football. And I was having fun doing something that I always wanted to do.

Chapter 11
New Passions

*A*S I MENTIONED PREVIOUSLY, I HAD FULL INTENTIONS OF PLAYING professional football for twenty years. It was definitely good money, and I loved doing it. However, once my grandfather Lynwood passed away at the beginning of the season in 2019, I didn't know if I wanted to keep getting up for the grind anymore. It just felt like it was time for me to stop and do something else.

The only thing I thought of doing after my football career was taking time off to relax and rest my mind and body. I didn't really know exactly what I was going to do next, but I felt like I needed to have a plan B. That was to become an actor. After having gotten my feet wet by doing a couple of small roles and cameo appearances, I started to think acting could become a full-time career for me. That was something I became really passionate about. The trick was for me to focus on figuring out a lane in that space.

The first thing I needed to do to steer myself into that new lane was to take time off from playing football. I had in mind that maybe I would take a year off, then come back and play more ball. However, after careful deliberation, I came to the decision that I wasn't coming back to play football at all. The time had come for me to hang it up and retire for good. There was no sense in playing the yo-yo game like so many other athletes did. I wanted to retire and stay that way. Besides, I had given my home city four good years of my career.

The truth is, during that final season I pretty much had a good idea of what I wanted to do. But I decided to wait until the season was finally over to start dealing with it. I chose not to talk about retirement openly or tell anyone. And I was recovering from a pretty strong concussion earlier on that year as well.

Behind the scenes, I was talking to doctors about my mental state, and they continued to examine me to make sure I was okay to keep playing. I figured my retirement wouldn't have surprised anybody after that, especially because I had already won a Super Bowl. Once the doctors gave me the okay, I went back to playing football. At the same time, I continued to think about hanging up my football cleats for good. I had one foot in and one foot out of the door. The doctors could certainly see my dilemma. It wasn't as if I was a rookie anymore. I had played for more than a decade in the sport with having sustained a lot of hits and injuries.

So, the doctors started asking me, "What do you want to do?"

I still hadn't come to my final decision, so I told them, "I don't know."

During the span of my professional career, I'd had several concussions, but that never made me feel like quitting. Once my grandfather passed away . . . that was different for me, and I wasn't feeling the same motivation to play anymore.

That's when the doctors first suggested, "Well, maybe you should consider hanging it up and retiring."

Everyone realized my football career was closer to the end than to the beginning. Most football players don't make it to forty. In fact, many players don't last fourteen years in the league, let alone *twenty*. Tom Brady is a very special man. Believe that!

There I was, contemplating retirement for that whole season of 2019. To walk away from the game after playing it for so long as the central focus of my life wasn't going to be easy. Then the team staff members started asking me about my future plans as well. I told them I'd talk about it once my contract was up at the end of the season. I did let them know there was a possibility of me not being interested in coming back. I remember my tight end coach, Pete Hoener, spoke to me about it personally. He was with me during my rookie year out in San Francisco, and he was now in Washington with the Commanders for that final year.

He asked me, "Hey, what are you going to do after this season in Washington? Do you have any interest in coming back?"

I told Coach Hoener the same thing I told the doctors: "I don't know, Coach. I don't know if I have interest in coming back anymore."

He was obviously trying to get me to keep playing. That's how coaches and managers do it. They bring you in. They talk to you and try to figure out what you want to do about joining the team, or rejoining.

"So, you don't want to play anymore? You're going to hang it up?" he asked me.

At that point, I figured there was no sense in my stretching out the process. So, I broke it to him. "Coach, I'm probably just going to hang it up, and keep it hung up."

He nodded to me and said, "Okay." Then he just looked at me without saying anything else. I guess he was trying to see how serious I was. If I wasn't playing anymore, there was nothing left to talk about.

His last words to me were, "I understand. I got you."

After coming clean about my plans for retirement, I did a few interviews on TV that confirmed it. I even did *First Take* with

Stephen A. Smith. The interview I remember the most, though, was this skit I did in Miami with a couple of other football players. I think it was right before I started saying anything about retirement. I initially thought I was doing this skit just for fun, but it ended up becoming my retirement announcement.

I had hooked up with Rob Gronkowski from the New England Patriots and James Harrison from the Pittsburgh Steelers, and we did a *Golden Girls* skit, like we were all old men. For the introduction, Rob Gronkowski said, "Welcome to Miami, the home of retirement. I brought my two friends with me, Vernon Davis and James Harrison."

Then we went into a skit on football retirement, which was pretty cool. It was also unexpected, because I didn't know my retirement was going to be announced before the Super Bowl that year. That's when San Francisco was back in it, with Jimmy Garoppolo at quarterback against the Kansas City Chiefs and Patrick Mahomes.

Once we did that skit in Miami, and they started airing it on TV, my retirement had pretty much been advertised for months. Then I went to the Super Bowl game in February 2020, and I was pretty much down there for my retirement. I made my rounds to speak to everyone I knew and respected, and I left right after the game and started to film another movie in Denver. This time, I was producing the film with my own company, Reel 85 Productions.

My team produced an action flick called *Red Winter*. It was a script that my buddy Marcus Smoot sent to me that we had plans to develop after I realized I was going to retire. So, I reached out to him and said, "Let's make this film."

I met Marcus through my buddy Kal Ross, who I've known since 2005. Kal is known for connecting you with like-minded people. Once I read the script from Marcus Smoot, I loved it! So, Marcus and I came up with a plan to shoot it during my offseason, because in my mind, I was still going back to play football for a few more years.

Marcus jumped right on it, and we got the writer involved, a guy named John Prescott. We pulled in another guy named Steven C. Pitts to direct, and Errol Sadler was one of the producers with my new film company who pulled all the pieces together. I have to give a bunch of credit to my guy Errol Sadler for getting it all done, because he had a lot of the infrastructure in place already. He had created a movie before we ever thought about producing one. All we had to do after getting the paperwork together was scout the locations and identify a line producer, who normally focuses on the numbers and the budget. The cast had already been identified because we knew exactly who we wanted for each role.

In the film, I portrayed the husband of a woman played by actress Ashley Williams, who witnesses a murder by two hit men out in the snow in Colorado. We were a couple in a rocky relationship who decided to take a ski trip together to try to work things out. However, when she witnesses the murder, of course the hit men want to kill her to destroy the evidence. So, it ends up being a run-and-fight-for-your-life, action film. I'm not going to tell you the rest of the story. You can still order the movie to watch online, or on a streaming service. The movie is on both BET Plus and Amazon Prime.

I recall we had to do casting over Zoom because COVID-19 had started to break out right before we shot the film. We didn't want to have all these people coming out to a public place to audition. It was too dangerous. The whole cast was pretty much people who had relationships with the production team and the crew. Then we had folks send in self-audition tapes while reading the script. The production crew was already highly interested in Ashley Williams because we knew what she could do.

With an action film like that, we didn't need to cast a lot of extras. There were only around ten of us in the movie and a couple of extras to round it out. We shot it in less than two months after my retirement. It was in February, right after I left the Super Bowl. We had everything set up already. I learned my lines in about fifteen days, and we shot the film, edited it in postproduction, and then we set up a meeting with BET Plus. They bought the film for their streaming network, and it came out two years later in 2022, and everybody loved it!

It took us a year to finish the film in postproduction, the most tedious part. It can take that long on average to fully complete a quality film, unless you already have guys editing while you're shooting it. Once the film was complete, the viewers thought it was a great film. We had a lot of realistic value added because of the snow and the natural backgrounds. That made it look authentic to the story, and it all came together nicely, with extremely cold weather, fight scenes, a lot of dialogue, and rented snowmobiles.

It only took us fifteen to twenty days to shoot everything and clear the locations that we needed to use in Colorado. We had everything taken care of as part of the production budget. My buddy Marcus was already a business-savvy guy who was just getting his feet wet in the film business, and so was I. It looked like my next direction in life as an actor was jumping off to a fast start.

I had already learned a great deal about acting while taking my first acting courses in San Francisco, where they emphasized important techniques for warming up before you perform. We all had to showcase our skills in a stage play at the end of the eight-week course to graduate from the class. In fact, we all had three performances, with a monologue and two stage plays. Everyone had to do that to graduate.

I was assigned a play called *Hurlyburly*. It was a movie from back in the day that had been adapted into a stage play. I had to perform with one female actress onstage while we both played our roles. Man, I just fell in love with the whole acting thing the same way I fell in love with my art studio—The Gallery 85—in San Jose.

I never owned the studio space, though. What I would do was rent it out on a month-to-month basis as I continued to feature new art. I even thought about bringing my art gallery idea back home to DC, but by the time I got home to play football for Washington, I had too much going on to do everything.

I had a great run with my art gallery out in California and I wanted to keep the Vernon Davis Foundation for the Arts going as a hub. I still wanted to support various charities and give back to the community so I could provide hope for those who were afraid to pursue their art as a real business. I wanted to show them that anything was possible, and they didn't have to be afraid to go all-out.

Then I changed the mission and approach to my foundation in 2016, when I reached all facets when it came to empowerment and providing opportunities to the young art movement. I wanted to take a more holistic approach to the Vernon Davis Foundation for the Arts, while focusing on health and well-being through scholarships, back-to-school supplies, eating healthier food, providing mentorship programs, and much more. So, I made my foundation all about leading the way and giving comfort to those who needed it, while helping kids to prepare better for what they could expect to deal with along the way to success. You know, because success is all a process.

Heading back home to DC at the end of my football career was perfect timing. I remember being at a point in my life where my focus had changed, and I had a lot of extra things going on. Those extra things included working hard to rekindle a relationship with my mother to try to get that right. That was still very important to me as soon as I realized I would be back home. My kids were older and bigger too, and I had to deal with a lot more of their needs in school, in life, and just in general.

With Janel no longer around as my girlfriend, I had to pay a lot more attention to the kids on my own as a single dad. Those were all the kinds of changes in my life that I had to adjust to and focus on.

I even acted in an independent cowboy movie called *Hell on the Border* when I first arrived back home in 2016. It was a film about Bass Reeves, the first Black deputy who served along the Mississippi River. I played a Black cowboy character named Columbus Johnson, who was transporting people from one side of town to the other. They traveled by wagons and horses in the era of the film, so I had to ride a horse in some scenes. I won't even lie to you: At first, I had a problem with riding a horse. I kept thinking, *I'm not about to ride no horse.* I had actually already ridden horses in real life out in California, though, so I manned up and killed it as a Black cowboy.

My first time riding horses was with a group of us in California. I faintly remember the details, but we were somewhere on a ranch. I remember being scared as hell at first. I mean, those horses were *big, strong, fast,* and *healthy.* I'm not sure how I did it, but I somehow mounted my 245-pound frame on this big, dark brown monster and went with it.

I had to press the same courage button that I pressed for everything else I had to do in life that scared me. Once I climbed up on this horse, though, I got into it and rode him for nearly two hours and covered a couple of miles. That was the only time I rode him, though. That must have been around 2012 or 2013. It was enough for me to have the horse-riding experience stored in my memory bank to ride a horse again in the cowboy role. And that's exactly what I did.

In fact, I took another acting course in DC around the same time that I did the *Baywatch* movie cameo. I found an acting coach named Robert Epstein, and I used to head over to his house every week for more training. He was referred to me by another buddy of mine, Jason Yorker, who I met during my University of Maryland years. He wasn't a student or teammate of mine, though. He was just a slightly older white guy who helped a lot of people out in the College Park community as a financial analyst.

I used to hang out a little bit and talk business with Jason when I first got drafted. It was just my luck that Epstein lived near us in DC, where I could work with him once I returned back home. I learned a lot of new techniques from Robert, and I've been working with him ever since. Hell, I'm still working with him now. However, there were times when I had to take a break from acting to focus on football. When I retired in 2020, I called him back, and we started working together regularly again.

That's around the same time that I started getting involved with the arts movement in DC. I became an active supporter of the young art talent in DC, just like I had in California, and I *loved it!* I even awarded gap scholarships to the art programs at the University of Maryland and Howard University. Overall, I was having some really exciting times back home. I was really involved in a lot of good things. I mean, I really felt good about where I was headed in my career after football.

I remember when we first started shooting *Red Winter,* and how we had to adjust to the COVID breakout. We started filming in late February but had to shut down production in March. At least we had gotten the majority of our winter snow scenes done. We were all on set when the pandemic hit, and I was scrambling around, feeling nervous after my costar, Ashley Williams, got sick.

Ashley didn't have COVID, but we didn't know that at the time because the pandemic was brand-new to everyone, and we were all just learning about the signs and symptoms. So, when Ashley became ill, I was in the hospital with her, just sitting there, and I really didn't know what was going on. I didn't even have a mask on yet because we didn't know all of the particulars of how to protect yourself. As more solid news began to pop up about the epidemic, we all learned more about the outbreak, and that's when things *really* got crazy.

People started flying out to the stores to buy bleach because you couldn't get any hand sanitizer. The stores began to sell out of it. And I mean, *everywhere!* I found myself running out like everyone else to buy bleach, gloves, masks, and all of the kinds of protective items we were being told to use. After the first few days, you couldn't even buy toilet tissue or paper towels. Those things were selling out everywhere. The pandemic was just out of control.

We had to reconvene and shoot the rest of the film in June down in Atlanta once things calmed down and we understood more about COVID. It took us about five days to reshoot with fifteen or sixteen people involved, from the actors, gaffers, production assistants, and everyone else. I remained excited and determined to get it all done. We were in *total* COVID protocol. Everyone had to get tested before they went on-site. You had to wear masks onset when you weren't performing. We actually had a COVID control officer, who showed up every week to make sure we didn't have an outbreak. Fortunately, we had pretty much already shot most of the movie in Denver in February and March. So, we just had a couple more pieces to film.

After producing that first film, I then produced *A Message from Brianna*. It was about this kid named Leonard, who grew up with his grandparents and had a girlfriend named Brianna who came to live with him for the summer. The girl then ends up missing, but it turns out that the grandparents were involved in something that their grandson didn't know about.

After this kid grows up, he actually moves back into the same house he had lived in with his grandparents. It was the same house where this girl, Brianna, was murdered. He buys the house, gets married, and has a daughter with his wife, but the spirit of Brianna is still inside the house, and she starts to possess his daughter. The married couple is then challenged to figure out a way to get the angry spirit out of their daughter and stay alive in the process.

Obviously, *Brianna* was a Black horror movie, and I played the lead role of the husband, Leonard. It was another ninety-minute film, like *Red Winter*, that I financed myself for $170,000. BET Plus paid us $550,000 for the rights to it. So, I tripled my return on the investment, and people said they enjoyed the film, especially my grandmother, Adaline. My grandmother enjoyed watching my movies a lot more than she did my football games because she knew that I was only acting in them, and I wasn't going to get hurt in a movie like I could in real life, playing football.

It was crazy how it all came about. I randomly met this guy, Deshaun Hardy in April 2020 through my business partner, Patrick Powell. He told me he had received an email from Deshaun stating that he was interested in working with me on a project. We met up to read and discuss the script. "You can play the lead," he told me.

Well, I liked what I read, especially because I was raised by my grandparents in real life. It was something I could totally relate to. I also liked the fact that I would be in control of getting it all done. That's what happens when you agree to produce a film with your own money. The completion of the film ends up being in your hands. My team came together again as producers on the project.

A Message from Brianna came out before *Red Winter* because *Brianna* took less time for us to edit. *Red Winter*, as an action movie, was a much more complicated film to edit, with more scenes and visual and audio details to work out. I didn't make as much on the first movie either. I remember the budget was a little higher, so the BET Plus rights payment wasn't as profitable.

After those first two films were shot, I stayed busy and jumped right in to perform on *Dancing with the Stars*. That was all in the same COVID year of 2020. I guess I wasn't that afraid of the pandemic because I never let it stop me from doing what I wanted to do. When the producers of *Dancing with the Stars* called me up, they said they had been trying to get me on their show for years.

I started talking to the casting director, Deena Katz, and she had reached out to me before, when I was in Sochi, Russia, for the Winter Olympics in 2014. I was there as an honorary captain for the United States curling team, and the producers of *Dancing with the Stars* contacted me through my agent. They wanted me to make a decision right away, but I was still playing football at the time. I didn't want to focus on dancing while still playing ball. It would've been too much for me. I like to stay focused on one thing at a time. So, I didn't do the show the first time I was asked.

Once I had retired from playing football, I was ready and willing to do it. You know, I was just looking to have fun. I no longer had to worry about playing football. I was so used to being active that I knew I just wanted to keep having fun. After that, I had a lot of different opportunities that came my way because people knew me from playing professional football. The popularity of football was opening up a lot more doors for me to walk through. I had made a name for myself.

So, when *Dancing with the Stars* called me again after my retirement, I was ready to go.

"I'll do it. Sign me up," I told them.

They liked picking athletic people, who were popular for their show. I guess I fit the bill: As a big guy they figured could move. Then they paired us up randomly with their dancers. They have somebody in their casting department who thinks up all that stuff and matches the dancers up with the talent. I ended up being paired with Peta Murgatroyd, who was amazing. I learned all of my dance moves from her. And it was hard! It was a tough process. I'm not the dancing type. I never even tried to explore dancing until they brought me on the show. That was definitely one of the toughest things for me to do. I had to spin her around and do all kinds of tough dance moves. We practiced a lot too, like three hours a day, *every* day. Then I would go home and practice for another hour and a half by myself to perfect my dancing for our show every Monday. I survived on the show for a good five weeks out of ten different celebrity dancers. Of course they take you off the show if you don't make it. We were all being graded. Overall, I think I did well. I made it to the halfway point.

After I got canned, though, I didn't watch the rest of the shows. However, I did make it a point to watch the end results to see who was still there and active to win. The dancing couple wins once they get down to the last three championship rounds. If I'm not mistaken, that's when you'll have three people competing against each other.

The rapper Nelly was on the show with me. AJ McLean, a singer from the Backstreet Boys, and Carol Baskin from the *Tiger King* show was on with me too. She was very popular. She might have been the most popular person on the show. Others who competed on *Dancing with the Stars* that season was basketball player Charles Oakley and the actress Anne Heche. May God bless her soul—she passed away in an accident in Los Angeles in August of 2022. I got pretty cool with her while we were filming. She was a sweet woman.

We also had Johnny Weir, the Olympic figure skater, on the show. I felt like Nelly should have won it, though. He made it all the way to the finals, but then Kaitlyn Bristowe from *The Bachelorette* ended up winning. I remember they started airing the shows around the end of August or early September.

I was busy as ever that COVID year. I retired from football and went right to work with everything else I wanted to do. I must have considered or worked on about thirty different projects after my retirement. You know, they just kept adding up as I went along. It was like one project after another. I knocked out so many projects. It just all started to add up over time, you know what I mean? After doing *Dancing with the Stars,* I got involved with another movie, *Gasoline Alley.* It was an action film, starring Bruce Willis, Luke Wilson, Devon Sawa, Kat Foster, and a model named Irina Antonenko.

We had a bunch of people in it. We even had the D.O.C. in there, you know, the rapper from N.W.A. I was given another role of a bouncer at a nightclub. It was a small role, but I was happy to be in it with those guys, you know, learning the trade. The people on the set get to know you too. When my new film manager, Henry Penzi, called me up and told me about the opportunity, I immediately said, "Yeah, let's go." But I think it was only released at select theaters and on video demand.

Henry kept finding me a lot of acting gigs and film production deals. I started working with him right after I retired from football. I already knew him before that, but once I retired, we started working together full time, and we just went to bat at making movies. We had deal after deal after deal, and commercial appearances as well. I actually did a few gigs while I was still playing football. I was in several commercials, but they weren't always endorsement deals. Sometimes I just jumped into projects that people wanted me to be in. It was fun. And I was just going with the flow. I had known Henry Penzi as early as 2016, so he really went to bat for me when we finally started working together. He kept me as busy as I wanted to be.

As for my grandmother, she was *loving* all of it. And that made me happy. However, I never got over the passing of my grandfather, Lynwood. I actually dedicated my Bruce Willis films to him, while remembering when we used to sit upstairs in his room and watch Bruce Willis movies. *Die Hard* was our favorite. Again, I owed getting to work with Bruce Willis to Henry Penzi. It was truly a blessing for me to work with him. I owe Henry a lot of credit for the success of my acting career, because he got me many exciting opportunities. We've done so much now that I can't even keep up with it anymore. I used to be able to keep track, but now I just do the projects and keep it moving. I'm still having a lot of fun with it.

Probably the biggest project I've ever done was being chosen as a judge on the Fox Network *Domino Masters* show, and then the movie role I got with Morgan Freeman.

We shot the *Domino Masters* show out in LA. It was crazy because the whole show was about toppling dominoes after building these giant platforms, with teams competing. I believe there were sixteen teams that came in. They had to build a world out of dominoes and then topple them after their structure was completed. Then we would judge who built the best creations and pulled off the best topple execution.

The teams had to try to execute a perfect topple with no stops in between. That meant the dominoes had to keep falling in flow the whole way around. I was on the show as a judge for fifty days or so. It was nearly two months and ten episodes. I had to judge based on the color scheme of the dominoes and make sure they were connected. We also judged the artistry and creativity of whatever the teams came up with.

I did that show in 2021, and it was one of the coolest jobs I've ever taken. The show had guidelines and rules for all the judges to follow. We even had different assignments as judges when we looked at other creative buildings. With the show being on Fox—one of the big four networks with CBS, NBC, and ABC—many people got to see it, including my grandmother and family. They paid me more to do it. So, it was an all-around sweet deal.

Then I did an independent movie with Morgan Freeman called *The Ritual Killer*. That was released both as a theatrical movie and was available for streaming from Redbox Entertainment. They bought the film rights to distribute it in the United States and Canada. Henry Penzi had sent my acting reel off to a producer he knew, and the guy offered me the role of Randoku, a twisted serial killer from South Africa, who was harvesting body parts. The character dealt with politicians and business-men, who would come to him when they wanted to feel power-ful. Based on what they needed, I would then take body parts from children and adults and mix them together with gold clay and herbs to blend it all into a brew called Muti. Sounds crazy, right?

I remember performing a scene while Morgan Freeman was on set. He was just standing there watching everything. So, I walked up and said, "How you doing, Mr. Freeman?" I made sure to be really respectful to him. I mean, Morgan Freeman was an acting legend. So, he shook my hand, looked at me with one eye, and then started joking around, as he always does.

"How are you doing, young man. You ready to have some fun?" he asked me.

Sometimes, he wouldn't say anything. He'd just wink his eye and start smiling. I came to know that Morgan is a real playful guy with a great sense of humor, but he's also one of the hardest-working actors I've ever seen or been around. At the time, he was eighty-four-years old. Can you believe that? Morgan was the oldest on the set, and yet he was the first to arrive and the last one to leave. He was very impressive, and he deserves all of the respect that he gets.

In the movie, he played a college professor who was helping this detective, played by Cole Hauser. Now, you can tell by *The Ritual Killer* title that the film was a suspenseful thriller. That's what Morgan is really known for now, outside of the award-winning *Glory* movie with Denzel Washington and *Driving Miss Daisy*, which Morgan starred in when I was still a kid. Since then, he's done a lot of suspense and thriller cop movies. Cole Hauser's detective character gets help from Morgan Freeman's college professor to help him figure out how to stop my witch doctor character from killing people. I probably got the role because of my football size and body.

It was another role Henry Penzi got for me after sending the producer my acting reel. I had to shoot many of the scenes with no shirt on and my chest out. I had never taken on a villain role like that before, but I wasn't afraid of it. After all, it was just a movie, and I liked to challenge myself, so I accepted the role and just did it. It wasn't really hard to me. Every role is tough if you don't apply yourself. But if you apply yourself and put the work in, you can accomplish it. That's how I've lived my whole life. It was the same thing I did with football. And, you know, I was excited to be in a scene with Morgan Freeman. I even had to choke him at the end. I didn't kill him, though. Instead, Morgan's character ended up stabbing me, enough to get me off him. The story still ends in a mystery, though. The college professor apparently sends Cole Hauser's character my eyeballs. He actually has my eyeballs delivered in a jar to him, but viewers never see Morgan Freeman killing my character.

That ending allows the audience to interpret the possibility of there being a couple of different conclusions. Maybe the college professor caught up with the ritual killer and did the world a favor by killing him. Another possible conclusion is that maybe this college professor used the killer as a scapegoat, and he's the real killer. You know, you could look at it several different ways. The final interpretation was pretty much left open-ended.

After completing the filming of this movie, I had a new relationship with Morgan Freeman. The whole time he was on the set, he was cool with me. He was such an amazing person and a real cool, hardworking guy.

I also had a nice relationship with Bruce Willis after being in two films with him, *Gasoline Alley* and *A Day to Die*—a video-on-demand movie that featured a lot of other stars in it. We had Just Leon from *The Five Heartbeats*, along with Kevin Dillon, Brooke

Butler, and a few other people. Bruce Willis played a crooked cop, while I played an ex-military guy who tries to help his friend save his family from syndicate hit men. It was really a great role for me because I got to act throughout the whole movie. I had a lot of different lines and screen time. That made me want to do *more* movies. I was *loving it*!

In the year 2022 alone, I think I acted in eight or nine projects. Most of them weren't theatrical releases, though. There's a lot of streaming movies coming out now, with all the different networks and streaming services. So, there are a lot more places to screen films for a supportive audience.

In addition to acting in films, I was still doing television game shows like *Name That Tune*. I ended up rapping on that show with a live band behind me and everything. The host, Jane Krakowski, challenged me to do it, and I was just having fun and being paid for it. That was another Fox Network show. It took about three days to tape a full episode, and we had to practice what we were going to perform beforehand. I was in Ireland for a week for that one. The first day on the set was just going through the logistics and getting familiar with how the game would be played, with the second and third day prepping and spending time hanging out in Ireland.

Then, I started thinking about being more selective in picking projects and shows to be involved in. I couldn't continue saying "yes" to everything. That's not to say I was a pushover who would do anything anyone asked me to do. I just wanted every role to be a good one for me, based on where I was in my life. As I began to put in my dues, I wanted to make sure that meant something for my progress and that I wasn't just standing still. You know, I wasn't a rookie in acting anymore.

Nowadays, I have some of my own projects and ideas to produce with Reel 85 Productions, and I try to always write them down. I've learned a great deal over the last few years. With the way audiences are now, watching more movies at home rather than going to the theater, it opened things up to create more content with lower budgets and fewer cast members.

Right now, I'm not all crazy about having theater distribution for my projects. We'll see what happens with some of my upcoming films. You never know. New projects on different levels are being pitched and developed every day. That's just the nature of any business that keeps going. Hollywood definitely keeps going.

So, what I do now is just let things come to me, while I continue to pick projects I like. I let them surface, and then wait for people to call me or Henry with the acting offers. In the process of advancing my career in acting and film production, I've also taken on a lot more commercials and television projects. Then I started thinking about writing a book about my life.

The first time I thought about writing my memoir was during that same busy COVID year of 2020. Even before that, I wondered about the process of writing a book while I was still involved in playing football. As a football player and professional athlete in general, you go through so many personal changes that you eventually think about documenting them. Along the way, you're given the opportunity to change your life in ways that probably wouldn't have happened otherwise.

Once you stop and think about it, where, you know, you played in a couple of Super Bowls, and everybody knows your face and your name, you figure you're qualified to write a book about it all. Athletes are even *more* popular in basketball and baseball because they don't wear helmets and facemasks, like football players do.

Then you think about boxers, tennis players, or golfers. Just think about how *big* Tiger Woods was all around the world for playing golf. My acting and producing in movies is similar to that. Now, I'm not anywhere *near* the Tiger Woods level of popularity, but it's similar in terms of more people from different walks of life getting a chance to see me do something different from what they're used to.

Rapping or singing can change your life and career like that as well. It's just a whole new world that opens up for you, especially if you're willing to take advantage of all of the opportunities that come your way.

Take me, for instance, hanging out and making movies with Bruce Willis and Morgan Freeman, all in the same year. At the time, I wasn't too concerned about Bruce's health. Maybe I should've been. I was just elated to be on the set with him. As a matter of fact, he seemed pretty normal to me. Would I have been able to do that had I not been a popular professional football player? Probably not. I would've had to pay my dues for another few years as an actor before I ever got an opportunity to meet all the different people and do the things that I'm now able to do.

I owe a lot of my success as an actor and movie producer to playing football, and the work effort that I put in to get where I wanted to be. Having a book published allows you to lock it all in, the things you were thinking, doing, and going throughout your life and career. At some point, I thought about putting it all together in a book. In a way, writing a book would be, like, a special gift to myself to remember it all, the journey that I've taken.

I remember I started reading motivational and self-help business books, like *Rich Dad, Poor Dad* by Robert Kiyosaki and *The Art of War* by Sun Tzu to keep my head right and be able to make wise decisions in my business dealings. Reading these kinds of books helped me to make the most of the business opportunities I got, which resulted in making more money. I also learned how to execute ideas more strategically.

When I was living in California, I used to go to this spacious Barnes & Noble bookstore just to hang out. It was a cool and quiet place to go. I felt really relaxed in the bookstore, and I liked it better than going to the library because all the new books equated to learning the new trends of business and marketing. It was so much more than just turning pages and reading. You had to know what was going on in the world of technology and how it was changing everything we do.

I also enjoyed looking at all the different merchandise that was being packaged, displayed, and sold. Being in this bookstore made me think of all the other interesting things I could get into, especially with millions of dollars in the bank. You know, I was always thinking about new business opportunities because, deep down inside, I knew I wasn't going to play football forever. And the money's not just going to sit there. You have to do something with it to make it grow.

So, I started telling my manager, my friends, family members, and anyone else, that it was now important for me to write a book. And I wanted to write one. But, you know, sometimes people hear you and think that you're just talking and not really serious until you actually do what you say you're going to do. That's exactly what you have managers for, to look into the things that you want to do and figure out a way to make those things happen.

Well, I was still playing football when the desire to write a book first came to me. I didn't have the time to start asking around about what I needed to do to write my book. So, I had my manager, Patrick Powell, to start asking for me. It actually ended up being Henry Penzi, again, who got me a book deal with the people and the connections he had.

He said, "I want you to come and take a meeting, Vernon. I have this group I want you to meet with about your book. Let's see if we can get a book deal." That happened with Henry right after my retirement year, once I got involved in making films and doing television. By then, I had more time on my hands to work on a book, and my football career was now over. So, we put the word out that I wanted to write a book about my life, and we waited to see what happened. And the rest, as they say, is history.

Coincidentally, my guy Henry also represents Rob Gronkowski, and we've hung out a few times together as popular tight ends who have won Super Bowls. Now Gronk and I have had some conversations about interesting projects in the works that *we* could do together. At six-seven, Rob Gronkowski is a big dude, who everyone knows likes to dance and have a good time. So, I could easily see us in a big-man comedy movie or a television show. Gronk and I have worked on a few things already, so only time will tell.

I've always had a busy mind and body that wants to do a lot of different things. When I came back to DC for good, I wanted to expand my horizons more. That's why I started to go to different schools, like the University of Maryland and Howard University, to give scholarships and funds to the art departments. I did several things like that. I even created a couple of projects on my own, such as Vernon's Closet, through my Vernon Davis Foundation, where I collected clothes from teammates and friends and then took them down to the Boys & Girls Club of Greater Washington. It was a joyful feeling to watch so many needy people come and select different garments.

Then I founded Read 85, a reading program that was adopted throughout the school system in the Washington, DC, area. What we'd do is collect eighty-five books to give away at the schools. We had people who would donate most of the books for the kids to read them. Within a month, if the kids read the books, they would be rewarded with grant money for college.

I still run all of my companies and foundations today. And I typically use my number 85 brand for most of them. I've come a long way since I first started my Vernon Davis Foundation in 2010 in San Francisco. Lately, I've been thinking about doing film projects that involve more young people in the District, like a skateboard film or another sports-related project. We have state-of-the-art skateboard parks all over DC now. I see them in different cities too. Right now, I'm just enjoying life, like a young DC skateboarder, having a blast just doing what I love to do.

As for the future . . . Well, let's just say . . . I've got some big plans . . . that I want to look into executing. I'll be sure to keep you guys in the loop.

Chapter 12
The Football Hall of Fame and Beyond

OF COURSE, IT'S EVERY FOOTBALL PLAYER'S DREAM TO BE INducted into the Football Hall of Fame after his career is over. That's when it's all about your numbers, your impact on the game, your team, and the position you played. It's harder for certain positions to go into Canton, Ohio, for a Hall of Fame bust than others. Once I started thinking about what my chances were, I did some research.

What I found is that only nine tight ends have made it to the Hall of Fame in its history. The list includes Tony Gonzalez, Shannon Sharpe, Dave Casper, Kellen Winslow, Ozzie Newsome, Jackie Smith, John Mackey, Mike Ditka, and Charlie Sanders.

From that list of tight end Hall of Famers, I like Tony Gonzalez the best because he could really stretch the field. He had a ridiculous wingspan radius to catch the ball with, and he was pretty efficient with his blocking in the run game. I think the most impressive thing about Tony Gonzalez is that he was consistent.

Tony put up consistent stat numbers and continued to be a matchup nightmare for opposing teams to cover. Many teams had a hell of a time trying to stop him in the passing game. He was a great route runner, but his biggest strength—in my opinion—was how he could stretch the field with his deep routes. Getting a big man deep down the field was very dangerous for winded linebackers or undersized safeties and nickelbacks.

Interestingly, Tony was never considered one of the fastest tight ends in the game when he played. But like Jerry Rice, he had a long stride and hustled down the field to create separation whenever you matched him up against slower or smaller defenders. Above all, he had great ball vision with soft, sure hands for a lot of great receptions.

A few new tight ends I expect to reach the Hall of Fame in the years to come start with Rob Gronkowski, of course. Then you have Antonio Gates from the Chargers, Travis Kelce—who's still playing with Kansas City—and Jason Witten from the Dallas Cowboys. You have to be retired for five years before you're eligible to go in. In my opinion, all four of those guys deserve it. Then I would have to make my own case in a few more years, after them.

When I reflect on the needs of the tight end position, I think about players who can catch passes *and* block. That's when you become a complete player and not just one-dimensional. I respect guys *more* when they can do it all and be selfless when they need to be. That's what Coach Mike Singletary conveyed to me.

The way I see it, you become an unstoppable player when teams have to figure out a defensive scheme just to slow you down in the passing game, while you still contribute to your team in the run game. In theory, you never have to leave the field unless you're injured or need a breather. When you can take your biggest and fastest player and force the defense to match him up with their best pass coverage defender—whether he be a linebacker, a safety, or a cornerback—you now can take advantage of other favorable matchups in the secondary. That's when you can make a name for yourself by being that valuable to your team.

Tony Gonzalez was that kind of tight end. He was also a great human being and a team player who put the needs of his team first when he played. A lot of pass-catching tight ends didn't like to block; they just wanted to catch passes. But Tony would block. I mean, he just evolved into the ultimate football player to me, and the perfect tight end. And his character was impeccable.

Basically, when you have a Hall of Fame–caliber tight end, that's when the defensive coordinators on every team have to sit down and put together a game plan to stop you, and that's what happened every year during my professional football career when I was at my best, and I still beat them. That's what makes a strong case for my acceptance into Canton, Ohio.

However, when I think about it, there's been hundreds of guys who played the position of tight end in the NFL, and less than ten of them have been elected to the Hall of Fame. In contrast, there's, like, twenty-one quarterbacks, twenty-four running backs, and thirty-five defensive backs.

On the flip side, there's only one punter, Ray Guy, and two kickers, Morten Anderson and Jan Stenerud, on the HOF list, and only seven centers. So, if you want the best opportunity to make the Football Hall of Fame, it's better to be like a Deion Sanders, Ronnie Lott, Ed Reed, and Charles Woodson type, playing defensive back. But really, that's like three positions: cornerback, strong safety, and free safety.

However, whenever I'm around my professional athlete buddies, and especially tight ends, like Rob Gronkowski or Antonio Gates, we never talk about the Hall of Fame. We just talk about football in general and reminisce about the games when we played against one another, and maybe talk about the new guys who are coming in and out of the NFL Draft.

In all, I had a great, productive football career, whether I

make it to the Hall of Fame or not, with two Super Bowl appearances and one win. I never broke 1,000 yards receiving in a season, but I scored more than a dozen touchdowns in a season
twice. At one point I was even number six all time for touchdowns scored by a tight end, which was a hell of an accomplish-
ment that I was very grateful to earn. Many tight ends have
never done that. At the end of the day, it's up to the people who
vote. So, I'm not going to lose any sleep over it. People know I
played, and it changed my life for the better, and Vontae's life as
well.

Right now, I just plan to keep on acting and producing movies,
giving back to my family and community, and inspiring people.
If I ever make it to the Hall of Fame one day, that'll be great.
And if not . . . I still had a great career, and I wouldn't change
anything about it . . . except for winning that first Super Bowl I
went to with San Franscico. I would have loved to come out of
that one with a win. We were that close to it.

I definitely think the National Football League Hall of Fame
is a wonderful reward for those who have played the game at a
high level and left everything they had on the football field,
like Kellen Winslow once did with the Chargers. I also think it's
a great goal for every ambitious player to keep in mind while
playing.

There have been a lot of players in the league who were really
good and made a huge impact on their team and on the game
who never made it to the Hall of Fame. Those are the guys we all
look at and say, "Gosh, he really should be in the Hall of Fame."

I certainly hope to be one of the next players the football fans
bring up in their Hall of Fame conversation in the future. After
such a long journey and football career, I learned that life is
about much more than me. It's about helping others and inspiring people to be the best versions of themselves. I did that by
showing resilience, determination, stamina, and by giving everything I had to give to challenge myself to succeed. I also sur-

rounded myself with positive, like-minded people, and I strongly encourage young people today to do the same.

A big key in life—I think—for anyone is to have support. Because without support mentally, physically, or spiritually, I wouldn't have been able to achieve some of the things I did in life. Having people like my pastor, my grandmother, and a bunch of great, supportive coaches was pivotal. But I had some good folks by my side when things got tough on me, because things will get tough in life, and it's all about how we *respond* to those things that determine whether we continue to have success in life.

You can either break down and give up when you're challenged or you can keep going with life's plans. This is especially true for the younger generations because you just don't know what they really are yet. Believe me, those challenges will surface for us all to make those hard decisions as we learn to stand the test of time. The way we do that is by relying on our faith and the great people in our lives while knowing that everything is going to be okay. That's what my faith, my family, and my friends have always told me.

I know I haven't talked about it much because people don't like to hear you preaching, but for me it was all about churches, churches, and *more* churches. I've always stayed close to a church, ever since I was a kid. Growing up with my grandmother, it was very important for us to go to church and keep the faith.

God was first and foremost in everything. As I continued to get older and my career began to evolve, I made sure that I kept a pastor near me to help navigate a lot of things that I needed to get through in life. Having that pastor's influence—especially when things got tough on me—allowed me to uncover the family roots that I learned from my grandmother, and that's to always try to help people, and do the right thing.

Acknowledgments

At the end of this very long process of completing my book, I'd now like to acknowledge all the people who have been true and dear to me, starting with my three children and all my family members: my kids, Jianni Davis, Valleigh Davis, Valaughn Davis, and their mother, Janel Horne. I want to thank Janice Braddock and the Braddock family. Again, I want to thank my grandmother and grandfather, Adaline Davis Smith and Lynwood Smith. I want to thank my mother, Jaqueline Davis, for all of her strength and my inspiration to succeed. I want to thank my brother Vontae, sisters Christina, Ebony, Veronica, and "Little Jackie." I want to thank my stepfather, Otis Willis, for all he did for me and the family. And we all continue to pray for and extend love to our brother Michael. I want to thank Aunt Patricia Davis, Uncle Mike, Aunt Sharon, Aunt Missy, Uncle Lloyd, and my whole extended Davis family. I want to thank my father, Vernon "Big Duke" Buchanan, my paternal grandmother and grandfather, James and Marguerite, Aunt Vanessa, Uncle Darren, and all of my Buchanan family. I want to thank my bro, David Simmons, cousins Shaneka Smith and Kadirdre McMillian, and all the rest of my family members, including the Ige family.

From my professional football years, I want to thank Coach Mike Singletary for showing me a better way and Coach Mike Nolan for putting up with me during my first few years in the league. I want to thank my guy Frank Gore and Coach Jim Harbaugh and the York family for getting us to the San Franscisco Super Bowl against Baltimore. I want to thank my offensive coordinator Norv Turner and tight end coach Pete Hoener. I want to thank my business partners, Patrick Powell and Michael Wright, my accountant, Suzanne Jones, and my financial adviser, Kharay Kenyatta. I want to thank my friends, teammates, and movie partners, Henry Penzi, Frank Deluca, Todd Stewart, Kevin Benton, Eric Shuster, DeShon Hardy, Brian Jennings, personal assistant Sasha Taylor, Jason Yorker, Moran Norris, Parys Haralson (RIP), Kal Ross, Robert Epstein, former mentor Amadou Tall, Dontae Hogan, Robert Armstrong, Alex Smith, Coach Greg Roman, Colt McCoy, Kirk Cousins, Wes Phillips, Scot McCloughan, Delaine Walker, Patrick Willis, and the whole San Francisco 49ers organization. I want to thank the Denver Broncos, with Peyton Manning, Brock Osweiler, and Demaryius Thomas (RIP, 2021). And I want to thank the Washington Commanders for bringing me back home to the DMV area.

I want to thank my whole Paul Laurence Dunbar Senior High School crew, my boys from Paul Public Charter Junior High School and Truesdell Elementary. I want to thank Coach Craig Jefferies, sports trainer Myron Flowers, Maryland head coach Ralph Friedgen, Shawne Merriman, D'Qwell Jackson, and the University of Maryland. I want to thank my best friend, Brandon Weekly, Josh Deckard, Ryan Nece, Pastor John Erwin, Jordan Reed, Bryant Young, and hundreds of other people who have helped me out along the way. I sincerely apologize to everyone I missed, but I didn't forget about you. I hold you deeply in my heart, which means way more than your name in a book.

Last but not least, I'd like to thank my writer, *New York Times* bestseller, Omar Tyree, my literary agent, Raoul Davis of Ascendant Entertainment, my Talent Manager, Timothy Beal of Universal Talent Bookings, my editor, Leticia Gomez, and the entire Kensington team. Thanks, guys! I really appreciate it. It's been a great ride and life journey to document.

Now let's go sell some books!

~ Vernon "The Real 85" Davis